MANAGING PUBLIC SERVICES

To the civil servants of Hong Kong

Managing Public Services

Crises and lessons from Hong Kong

AHMED SHAFIQUL HUQUE
GRACE O. M. LEE
City University of Hong Kong

Ashgate

Aldershot • Burlington USA • Singapore • Sydney

Published by
Ashgate Publishing Limited
Gower House
Croft Road
Aldershot
Hampshire GU11 3HR
England

Ashgate Publishing Company
131 Main Street
Burlington, VT 05401-5600 USA

Ashgate website: http://www.ashgate.com

British Library Cataloguing in Publication Data
Huque, Ahmed Shafiqul
    Managing public services : crises and lessons from Hong
    Kong. - (Social and political studies from Hong Kong)
    1. Civil service - Management 2. Communication in public
    administration 3. Crisis management in government 4. Civil
    service - China - Hong Kong - Management - Case studies
    5. Communication in public administration - China - Hong
    Kong - Case studies 6. Crisis management in government -
    China - Hong Kong - Case studies
    I. Title II. Lee, Grace O. M.
    351.5'125

Library of Congress Control Number: 00-134822

ISBN 0 7546 1128 0

Printed and bound by Athenaeum Press, Ltd.,
Gateshead, Tyne & Wear.

Contents

Preface

The management of public services is an increasingly difficult task. Providing public services of an acceptable quality on a regular basis is an intimidating responsibility. This has been further complicated due to ever-increasing demands in the face of a decreasing allocation of funds for producing and delivering such services. Furthermore, rapid changes taking place in societies calls for new skills and the innovative application of knowledge to the problems of public organisations. Generally, traditional bureaucratic organisations find it difficult to deal with the increasing demands imposed upon them by the changing circumstances.

While routine management of public services is a major challenge, encountering crises in the form of non-routine problems makes public managers' lives even more difficult. The operation of public agencies cannot be expected to continue in a routine and expected manner. New services are required, demands have to be faced and responded to, activities do not proceed as planned, and problems emerge in unexpected places and at unusual times. No matter how critical a new problem is, public managers have to respond to such deviations from their regular pattern of work, and continue to provide public services.

Hong Kong provides an interesting background for exploring the issue of managing crises in the area of public management. The ever-expanding scope of public services management includes several tangible and intangible activities, and both types are equally important. While some activities are concrete in nature and can be appreciated in the form of better physical facilities and direct services such as medical care and education, others are somewhat obscured from public view. Yet, the importance of ensuring that the public have full confidence in the government and its commitment to transparency, maintaining open channels of communication between the government and the governed, and reaffirming the effectiveness of the rule of law in a country are not always fully appreciated by authorities. Consequently, these important areas of public management are often relegated to the background, as organisations emphasise areas that produce visible and quantifiable results. In focusing on the provision of concrete and tangible output in the form of public services, governments may often neglect the intangible services that must also be provided to the public.

Poor performance in the provision of the intangible public services can contribute to major crises in public organisations. This book examines four such cases in the context of the rapidly changing political and social environment of the new Hong Kong Special Administrative Region of the People's Republic of China. In the wake of its reversal of sovereignty to China, a number of crises were encountered in the management of public services in Hong Kong. While some of these might have been tolerated as an occasional lapse of judgement or administrative error/oversight in the past, a democratically inclined polity and socially conscious public took notice of the perceived threat to transparency, open communication, and the rule of law and the poor performance by senior public servants. These events are, therefore, recognised as "crisis", and efforts are made to explain their causes and consequences, and to compile a list of lessons to be learned from the experience.

This book is the outcome of a long period of planning and contemplation, although the end product had to be prepared in a relatively short period of time. The literature on managing crises in public organisations is rather limited and that was one of the principal reasons for undertaking this study. The use of recent cases from the public sector in Hong Kong will help readers understand the difficulties faced by modern governments in providing basic services to the public, along with fulfilling the responsibility of establishing trust and confidence in a new government framework.

This study was made possible through a strategic research grant from the City University of Hong Kong. We would also like to acknowledge a debt of gratitude to Lisa Wei-yee Wong. She has been an excellent contributor to the study and diligently collected material on the cases. Her insight has been extremely useful in understanding and analysing the crises outlined in this book. Thanks must also be expressed to Ms. Jessie Wai-Ki Lui for her assistance with word-processing.

Professor Paul Wilding of the University of Manchester provided valuable advice from the inception of the study. He has been a source of constant support and encouragement throughout the period of study and has won our admiration as a superior human being. We are also grateful to our colleagues in the Department of Public and Social Administration at the City University of Hong Kong for helpful comments and suggestions received. The School of Business and Public Management at Victoria

University of Wellington, New Zealand, helped by providing access to facilities for several weeks.

Thanks are also due to a number of friends and colleagues who provided help, advice and encouragement throughout the manuscript's preparation. We would like to mention Muhammad Yeahia Akhter, Jonathan Boston, Bob Gregory, John Martin, Pat Walsh, and Habib Zafarullah in this regard.

We would like also to register our deepest regards for our spouses - Yasmin and John - and appreciation for our children - Shineen, Ariqa, Jane, and Edward.

We, however, remain responsible for any shortcomings of the study.

Ahmed Shafiqul Huque
Grace O.M. Lee

1 Managing Public Services

Events of the past year have tested civil servants' responsiveness and ability to manage crises. We must and we will strive to do better. The community expects nothing less than full dedication and professionalism from its public servants.

Address by the Chief Executive the Honourable Tung Chee Hwa to the Legislative Council Meeting, October 1998

The Management of Public Services in Hong Kong

The management of public services has emerged as a major challenge to modern governments. As societies and communities develop and are exposed to external influences, the diversity and volume of demands are exacerbated, and governments are forced to respond in the interest of social stability and human development. Consequently, a variety of strategies are adopted to reduce expenses, seek help from the private and non-profit sector, and streamline the management and operation of public organisations. Different countries adopt strategies on the basis of ideology, level of development achieved, technological capability, and the effectiveness and inclination of the bureaucracy and society, in order to deal with the growing challenge of providing pubic services.

In view of developments in various countries around the world, the efficient and effective management of public services is viewed as one of the crucial tasks of governments. While there are constant demands for the provision of increased and better services for citizens, financial constraints make that task more challenging. Democratisation and globalisation have opened up opportunities for public scrutiny and participation in the production and delivery of services. Such developments have also had an impact on their operation and performance, as time and resources have to be allocated to anticipate and to respond to questions both inside and outside the legislature. The changes that have been taking place in Hong Kong over the past decade have had a significant impact upon the nature, orientation and operation of public services.

Hong Kong has been returned to China, with worldwide attention having been riveted upon the preparation, the handover itself and beyond.

There is a high degree of interest regarding the continuity of government and administration in the new Special Administrative Region of the People's Republic of China, and Hong Kong's ability to hold on to the competitive advantage enjoyed by the territory for a long time. At the same time, the transformation from an outpost of the British Empire to an eminently important region of China is worth particular attention. Administrative systems generally have a difficult time coming to grips with rapid and major changes, and even the most stable would show signs of instability when faced with the kind of complex environment Hong Kong has encountered.

There was a demonstration of considerable interest in the development and future potential of Hong Kong in the days leading up to its handover back to China. A wide range of publications examines pre-handover developments in Hong Kong's social, political, legal and administrative arrangements. While economic development has received extensive treatment, a fair amount has also been produced on the social and political aspects of development (see, for example, Burns, 1994; Cheng, 1986; Scott, 1989; Miners, 1995; Lethbridge, 1978; Rabushka, 1973; Li, 1997; and Wesley-Smith & Albert Chen, 1988). Few of these studies present in-depth analysis of the role of the institution of the Civil Service and the administrative system, which have made significant contribution to the economic, social and political development achieved by Hong Kong.

As the dust begins to settle after the handover, it is becoming evident that Hong Kong will be facing formidable challenges in a number of areas in its efforts to maintain the presently enjoyed competitive edge over its rivals. While much will depend on the management of Hong Kong's relationships with the People's Republic of China and the international community, as well as the economic system, an efficient management of the public services is of equal importance. The Civil Service plays an extremely important role in running Hong Kong, and participates in all major decisions regarding economic, political and social policies. The implementation of such policies also depends, to a large extent, on the ability and co-operation of civil servants. The delivery of public services is intimately related to the processes preceding it, and the nature, quality and consequences of managing them have come to constitute a core element of the process of good governance. Hence there is a need for a study to examine the nature and role of civil servants and their efforts to ensure continuity amidst the numerous changes taking place in Hong Kong, with reference to the production and delivery of public services.

The Background

Despite gloomy predictions over the future of Hong Kong after 1997, the city has retained a position of great significance in the Chinese political system, as well as in the international community. Hong Kong continues to hold full membership of a number of international organisations, while it seeks to make useful contributions to the developments taking place within Greater China. It remains one of China's major cities, as well as a key business and financial centre in the Asia-Pacific region. Quality of life has improved continuously over the past three decades and social and political developments have made the management of public services a demanding task.

Hong Kong's civil servants have been trained and oriented in the British colonial tradition, although preparations have been afoot for some time to adjust their attitude and outlook, and re-orient them to help cope with the various challenges that are likely to be confronted by the public service (Huque & Lee, 1996). A number of new developments in Asia in general, and Hong Kong in particular, point to the need for an assessment of the preparations made and capabilities attained to meet the challenges faced by the Hong Kong SAR after its reintegration with China. There is concern across Asia, and elsewhere, over the issues of democratisation, economic growth, marketisation, globalisation, political participation and human rights. Many of these hinge upon the relationship and interaction between governments and citizens. The management of public services acquires increased importance in view of the fact that they serve as a basic indicator of the relationship between the public and the government.

The apparent success of Hong Kong over the past three decades is reflected in a number of outcomes. Three elements have played a key role toward economic development in Hong Kong: "the state of the world economy, the territory's ability to compete in international markets and its skill in attracting overseas investment" (Huque, Tao & Wilding, 1997, p. 2). The Civil Service, one of Hong Kong's key institutions, "has been credited with the accomplishment of a number of tasks which have contributed significantly to the success of the tiny territory in becoming a major trading and commercial centre and in its reputation for efficient and effective service provision" (Huque, Lee & Cheung, 1998, p. 6). In providing welfare services, the government of Hong Kong adopted the practice of developing five-year plans for social welfare development. The Plan is reviewed periodically "to assess the extent to which services are effectively meeting the respective policy objectives, monitor the progress of the implementation of agreed plans for service development, determine specific targets of expansion for each service over a five-year period, and identify possible areas for change and improving the effectiveness of the service" (Government of Hong Kong, 1995, p. 1).

The provision of public services has thus continued to assume great importance in the operation of the government in Hong Kong. The government has established itself as a provider of some of the most essential services to the community, as well as the facilitator for several more. The community has responded to these services with increased levels of consumption and an enhanced aspiration that has exerted pressure on the providers. The Civil Service, as the main instrument for the provision of public services, has also been brought under the spotlight with the objective of assessing its performance and improving the quality of the public services. A combination of these factors makes the study of the processes and outcomes of the management of public services a worthwhile undertaking at this juncture in the history of Hong Kong.

This book seeks to examine the task of the management of public services in Hong Kong, with reference to recent local developments. Public services are provided in Hong Kong by a large group of civil servants, who are selected through a stringent process of recruitment. They proceed through their careers by demonstrating their competence in specific areas, and well-designed training programmes enhance their capability. The government embarked on a systematic training programme to enhance its civil servants command of the important languages - Cantonese, English and Putonghua - and organised orientation programmes to familiarise them with the society and government in China. A programme of localisation was undertaken to replace expatriate officials with those better equipped to deal with local problems and are committed to the development of Hong Kong.

However, a number of weaknesses became evident soon after the handover, when Hong Kong faced a series of management crises. Within the short period of ten months, public sector managers in Hong Kong had to deal with a variety of major problems. Even before the handover took place, a controversy emerged with the resignation of the Director of the Immigration Department, who was allowed to leave the service after an exceedingly short period of notice. The case led to questions about the procedures behind, as well as the reasons for the resignation, and the government came under attack from various quarters for the manner in which the case was handled. The issue became even more complicated when the resigning official was elected as a member of the Preparatory Committee for the return of Hong Kong to China. An analysis of this case is expected to provide useful insights into the issue of transparency in the management of Hong Kong's public services.

Soon after the handover, several risks to public health posed further threat to the reputation of the SAR's public managers. The handling of the "bird flu" crisis led to questions about the ability of the post-handover Civil Service to manage emergencies in an efficient manner, and confidence was further damaged by several errors in public hospitals and a surge of "red tides" that threatened to contaminate local fish stocks. Other related cases include the detection of E-coli bacteria in beef, and pesticides used in the production of vegetables, which adversely affected a number of residents. This study will focus on the detection of the "avian flu" virus and the management of the resulting crisis that culminated in the slaughter of a huge number of chickens. The case involved certain steps by the poultry industry aimed at risk avoidance, but also required governmental action to minimise public risk (for details, see Shrader-Frechette, 1991).

In addition to the government's personnel problems and the threat to public health just mentioned, the legal department was confronted with a serious challenge over the prosecution of three senior staff of the local *Hong Kong Standard* newspaper. While one of its major shareholders was named as a co-conspirator in attempts to defraud the government, she was excluded from the charge sheet when it was finally prepared. The prominent position held by the co-owner and her close association with the Chief Executive, as well as with leaders in China, gave rise to speculation over the effectiveness of the judicial system. An examination of this case will reveal interesting information on the effectiveness of the rule of law in the new SAR and, at the same time, raise awareness about the level of transparency in the operation of government.

Following the rapid growth experienced by Hong Kong during the 1970s and 1980s, it was decided that the territory needed a new airport that would be capable of handling the predicted air cargo and passenger traffic, as the existing Kai Tak Airport was expected to reach its capacity by 1995. The new airport, to be located at Chek Lap Kok, was considered essential to welcome more visitors, relieve Kowloon residents of noise pollution, retain Hong Kong's status as an international and regional centre of aviation, as well as to boost the process of development (Patten 1992, p. 11). The planned airport was to be one of the best and biggest in the world and was scheduled to be completed before the handover in 1997. Its opening proved to be anti-climactic, as a number of problems affecting operation emerged on the first day. It seemed inconceivable that a project with the huge amount of investment involved could be faced with such problems, and the government initiated investigations along with the Legislative Council and the Ombudsman. This case will be studied to underline the importance of co-ordination, communication and attention to the smallest detail in providing public services.

Hong Kong had been reeling from one crisis to the next, when the most potent force, an economic crisis, hit it. While other Asian economies were succumbing to the combined effects of regional turbulence, local leaders presented a calm front suggesting that Hong Kong would not be affected, since fundamentals were strong and the government had followed prudent money management policies. By the end of the second quarter of 1998, it was clear that a crisis was imminent, and various measures to deal with it were being contemplated by the government. While the government kept a brave face, the economic crisis had resulted in the sharp decline of the stock market index, the closure of businesses, widespread lay-offs and a steep rise in unemployment. In spite of initial attempts to stimulate the economy and promote growth, the problem was ignored for a period as the government went into denial and sought to buy time to understand and deal with the crisis. However, in a desperate effort, the government abandoned its long-preferred policy of "positive non-intervention", and invested massively to bolster the local stock market (see Huque, 1999). The effort, in spite of drawing criticism from several quarters, resulted in a return of stability to the financial market and the Hong Kong government reaped enormous profits from the endeavour. While for some time it appeared that another crisis might have been precipitated, the stock market has bounced back and the strategy seems to have succeeded. The handling of the economic crisis will not be explored in this study, but may be used to highlight management problems of the other cases.

Some of the unexpected events and problems described above will be used for examining the management of Hong Kong's public services. Using a case-study approach, this book will examine various aspects of administrative management, which is expected to shed light on the origin of the problems and efforts by the government to deal with them. This exercise will indicate the adequacy of preparation taken before the handover, the impact of some of the steps taken in the process, and suggest ways and means for the future.

The Context and Environment

Public service management may be interpreted in several ways. The problem stems partly from the definition of the term. In several studies, the term "public service" is used synonymously with "Civil Service", and to denote "those white-collar, generally nonprofessional, career personnel who have tenure and who are administered according to traditional Civil Service practices; its overriding characteristic is the emphasis that is placed on the *position*; its description of duties, responsibilities, requirements, and qualifications" (Henry, 1999, p. 287). In keeping with such an approach, public service management could denote the task of managing the large number of public officials who are appointed to positions in governmental agencies. These activities are usually carried out by a number of agencies including the Public Service Commission, a department of personnel or Civil Service, and such bodies.

However, public organisations are engaged in providing a number of services to citizens. These cover a wide range and include the maintenance of law and order, the collection of revenue, ensuring the preservation of fundamental rights of citizens, allocation of goods and services, provision of adequate facilities for the operation of the private sector, and many more tasks and responsibilities. In short, public organisations provide services to ensure that citizens are free from harm, are able to pursue their professions and objectives in life, and are expected to assist their clients in the pursuit of those objectives. Naturally, a number of skills and strategies are required in managing public services, since they are offered with a diverse range of objectives.

This study encompasses certain aspects of both of these interpretations of the concept of public service. The products and services as well as the public organisations themselves contribute towards many outcomes. On the one hand, they provide citizens with freedom, security, access to facilities, health care, education, recreation, and other necessities of life. On the other hand, public services help to establish the trust and confidence of the citizens in the system, by ensuring equal treatment for all through the application of rule of law, and engaging in activities to establish its transparency and effectiveness.

The cases in this study will place selective focus on the transparency of public personnel management, confidence of citizens in the legal system, ability to provide a reliable health service, and the capability to operate major public facilities. To achieve these ends, an in-depth examination will be made of the government's attempts to deal with four crises - the resignation of the Director of the Immigration Department, the outbreak of avian flu, the prosecution of the staff of a local newspaper (the *Hong Kong Standard*), and the problems encountered on the first day of operation of the new Hong Kong International Airport.

Crises in Public Organisations

Similar to all other organisational arrangements, public services are compelled to operate under a number of guidelines and constraints. The legal and constitutional framework of the country, the public nature of the organisation, and the constantly changing demands and pressures emanating from these sources create a formidable challenge. Public managers are generally recruited on the basis of merit and are expected to faithfully and routinely apply rules and regulations in making decisions in producing and delivering public services.

Any unforeseen or unexpected event, and even some of those anticipated, can precipitate crises. The magnitude may be great or small, the implications may be widespread or limited, but the challenge to public management remains formidable. In cases of events affecting a small number of citizens or groups thereof, public services can act swiftly and decisively to deal with crises. But the very nature of public services affects the way in which crises are handled. The problem starts with the definition and identification of a crisis.

Rosenthal, Hart and Kouzmin view crises as something that refers "to serious threats to basic social, institutional and organizational interests and structures. Moreover, fundamental values and norms can also be threatened. From an administrative point of view, crises necessitate critical decision-making under conditions of time pressure and considerable uncertainty" (1991, p. 212). Hence, not only do crises put pressure on public managers through the presentation of an unexpected scenario, but add to that stress by imposing various other limitations on them.

For example, public servants have a number of constraints under which they have to operate. The time available for collecting, assessing and analysing information, and the freedom of choosing the best decision to deal with crises are not present (see Simon, 1957). As a result, public managers choose strategies that will cause the least disruption or pressure in their scheme of operation. Generally, the managers have a set of tasks and responsibilities assigned to them. They encounter routine problems in the daily course of their work, and develop routine or programmed responses to them.

A different situation arises when the challenges are out of the ordinary, i.e. different from the routine problems. Most public managers, particularly those at the middle and lower levels of the hierarchy, find these difficult to handle. Owing to the rigid hierarchical nature of public organisations, decision-making authority is not sufficiently decentralised to allow these officials to respond to the circumstances, make a quick decision and deal with the problem.

Senior-level public service managers suffer from other complications. They, too, are unprepared to embark on the task of making a quick decision to deal with non-routine problems. Their orientation and training in the public service have instilled a culture of procrastinating over a problem, with the expectation that it will disappear or resolve itself. A non-routine response also carries the danger of indicating that the established plan and practice for dealing with all possible scenarios is ineffective.

Do non-routine events generally constitute a crisis in the public service? If the public officials are unable to respond quickly, even an apparently insignificant event can blow up into a major crisis. Obviously, a situation that draws attention to specific problems of a non-routine nature calls for a solution which will also be of a non-routine nature. While in some cases these assume the dimension of a crisis, the situation may still be under control in others, as long as public trust and confidence in the government and the system is not jeopardised.

It is also necessary to consider the approach taken in training and orientating public officials for discharging their duties. In most cases, the training is task orientated. Officials are helped to develop skills and techniques required to perform regular duties. Most training programmes also include elements for developing intellectual and thinking capability. During the 1970s and 1980s, increased emphasis was placed on the importance of educating public officials in ethical issues. While these developments have served to make public management more relevant to the needs of the times, to some extent a significant area appears to have been neglected in the preparation of managers. This refers to the basic values of the management of public services, such as upholding the rule of law, transparency and openness, and the promotion of a positive image of public organisations.

This argument is relevant to crises and their management in public organisations. Crises erupt not only from the emergence of a situation in which something has gone wrong or the recognition of circumstances which cannot be responded to according to established practices and procedures. Occasionally, minor problems can be blown up into crises due to an inability to handle them efficiently or to the lack of attention to the comprehensive role of public managers. In this way, a fallout of issues related to the resignation of a public official or a limited number of breakdowns at the opening of a major infrastructure can accumulate to acquire the nature of a crisis. Therefore, the management of public services needs to consider all aspects in formulating action to deal with a crisis. This points to the need of recognising the basic values of public service management in preparing personnel, managers and the government to deal with crises in an effective manner.

Public officials prepare for serving the country through pre- and post-entry training and orientation for their jobs. Usually they are prepared for performing specific tasks that are directly related to the output of the organisation. Such skills are essential for every public official to demonstrate their utility, and are considered in appraising their performance. Thus, for example, an official serving in the health sector will have the knowledge and skills to undertake tasks that could be, in the end, related to an increase/decrease of citizens seeking health care, to the number of patients successfully treated in public hospitals, or even to lowering the amount of allocations required to meet the needs of patients. But there is an intangible output from public organisations that is not easily measurable and often neglected in the appraisal of public officials. In this way, the actions (or inaction) of public officials may enhance or erode the confidence of the public in the system or present the government in a negative light. To citizens, the front-line officials often represent the government, and they need to be aware of the implications of the intangible output of public organisations. Without such a comprehensive approach to the management of public services, the risk of relatively minor problems blowing up into full-scale crises will be high. In the end, this could add to the high cost of providing public services.

Fearn-Banks defines a crisis as "a major occurrence with a potentially negative outcome affecting an organization, company, or industry as well as its publics, products, services or good name" (1996, p. 1). Fink views a crisis as a turning point in any situation that runs the risk of escalating in intensity, falling under close media or government scrutiny, interfering with the normal operations of business, jeopardising the positive public image presently enjoyed by a company or its officers, or damaging a company's profitability (1986, p. 15).

Although these definitions of crisis are couched in terms of circumstances pertaining to the private sector, they also help identify and understand crises in the public sector. It is conceivable that the magnitude of the problems and their impacts will be much greater in public services. Not only are the consumers of public services larger in number, but the stakes are much higher. The wellbeing of citizens, the legitimacy of the government and the fate of the polity rest on the quality of the management of public services.

A Framework for Analysis

Understanding and analysing crises in managing public services entails an appreciation of the numerous constraints under which public organisations operate. The agencies are established through legislative action, receive the resources necessary for operation from the central government following stipulated procedures, are accountable to the community as well as to the representatives of the people, and risk cutbacks in the event of failure or adverse public opinion.

Managers in the public service are given responsibilities in specific areas of activity, with the knowledge that they might have to move to another assignment at short notice. Most are generalists who have acquired a broad base of experience serving in various agencies. This group is extremely adept at making managerial decisions of a regular nature, but often lacks depth of knowledge and information in the face of non-routine situations. Without specialised knowledge of the area in which a problem emerges, senior managers have to seek expert advice before making critical decisions.

Another problem area in public organisations is the authority of making decisions at the point of crises. While crises call for immediate decisions and quick action, the strict hierarchical nature and rigid framework of operation of such organisations invariably results in delays. Messages and communications have to travel up and down the hierarchy, making stops at the prescribed points, before a decision can be considered to have been taken in an appropriate manner. Meanwhile, the extent of a crisis escalates and causes harm and discomfort to the public.

The issue of jurisdiction has always been contentious in public organisations. Government departments are entrusted with responsibilities that may overlap with one another. For example, the department of agriculture may be concerned with - in addition to the production of crops - input, transport, marketing, export, regulation and many other areas. Obviously, some of these activities must be conducted in co-operation with the departments of customs and excise, trade, industries, transport, etc. At times of crises, jurisdictional problems may emerge as major obstacles to tackling them. Inter-departmental co-ordination in making decisions and their implementation may prove costly in terms of delays, and impede the adoption of the most rational strategy for dealing with problems.

Finally, crises often loom larger than they actually are. The perception of the public is shaped by the government's responses. If the public managers appear to be shaken and unsure of their strategies, the crises assume greater magnitude in the perception of the public. They feel insecure and cannot understand the reasons for the public organisations' failure to contain the crisis and the resulting damage. The public does not expect these organisations to be in complete control over their areas of operation at all times. However, problems not presented in the proper context and a lack of communication from the government on its intentions, can be viewed as signs of weakness and helplessness. A high degree of transparency in keeping the public informed of problems, their possible solutions, and the action being taken by public organisations, can go a long way toward alleviating the anxiety of citizens, and can serve as a crucial first step in managing crises in the public sector.

Identifying and Managing Crises

Identifying a crisis in public management is a critical task. Often, public service managers are unable to recognise a crisis situation, or worse, are unwilling to accept the reality. Steeped in the tradition of bureaucratic management, they adopt a "wait and see" approach, and hope the crisis resolves itself. Rosenthal and Kouzmin (1997) have developed a "five-step framework" to establish a "political setting" to assist with governmental decision-making. The framework also helps to define what components are needed before an event can be perceived as a crisis. They go on to specify five steps, the first three of which help to determine if a serious threat to the social-political system exists, the necessity to respond to that threat, and the need for government decisions. The decisional issue highlights the next two steps. "The fourth heuristic step in understanding, even shaping, possible governmental crisis decision making involves the necessity for prompt decision making by government authorities" (1997, p. 293). The fifth step "involves the transition from an external observation of the necessity for government authorities to engage in crisis decision making to the authorities' perception that they should, indeed, make critical decisions at short notice" (1997, p. 295).

It is important that public managers have the ability to identify potential threats to the existing framework for administering and delivering public goods and services. The symptoms may emerge as small failures in particular areas of operation or major flaws in the policy framework. Sometimes, "what some might perceive to be a self-evident crisis, may, in fact, be an event perceived differently by other agencies, actors and interest groups" (Rosenthal, Hart & Kouzmin 1991, p. 212). The interdependence of public organisations and the complexity of relationships often prevent the identification of potential crises. The routine handling of a case by immigration official may give rise to critical consequences regarding fundamental rights or accountability.

The identification of potential crises in itself is not an end. Public managers must realise the need to respond to the crisis (or potential crisis) and act accordingly. Public organisations face numerous constraints in initiating a response to an event of an unusual nature. Before action can be taken, they must convince themselves and other stakeholders of the potential threat to the system, and this is not easy. Moreover, as public managers must operate under the guidance of the political executive, they must obtain unqualified support from that group. Few public officials, except those located at the top echelons of the hierarchy, have the means, ability or authority to act in the face of crises.

This issue is intimately related with decision-making patterns in public organisations. By design, the power to make major decisions is concentrated at the highest levels of public organisations. In spite of repeated calls for delegation and decentralisation, sufficient authority has not been installed at other levels of such organisations to enable middle and lower level managers to act swiftly. The centre retains considerable power on the pretext of co-ordination and standardisation, and officials at the lower levels are deprived of the opportunity to participate in making decisions that they are required to implement.

Similar problems impede the management of crises in public organisations. Terry identified four approaches to public management (1998), and these can be applied to the analysis of crisis management. The quantitative/analytic approach emphasises "the strategic use of sophisticated analytic techniques such as forecasting and cost-benefit analysis", while the political management approach "assumes that public managers have a legitimate right to exercise political power in the policy making process" (Terry, 1998, p. 195). In the other two approaches, "liberation management" advocates the idea "that public managers are highly skilled and committed individuals who already know how to manage", and "market-driven management" suggests "that public managers will increase their performance levels if exposed to market forces" (Ibid).

Generally, the quantitative/analytic approach appears to be the most suitable in managing crises in the public services. Combined with the assumption of liberation management, it can be expected that skilled and committed public managers would apply sophisticated techniques to anticipate and respond to crises and continue to provide public services at the desired level. However, such assumptions fail to recognise the issue of political management. In most cases, public managers are unable to exercise political power, and have to abide by decisions (or non-decisions) made by the political executive. Consequently, in a polity like Hong Kong, where the public managers are highly visible, the burden of responsibility shifts to the public service. As Rosenthal, Hart and Kouzmin (1991) put it, "crisis management and crisis decision making involve many actors in the political-administrative sphere", including politicians as well as bureaus and bureaucrats, and bureau-politics plays an important role "in the planning, response and post-crisis stages of crisis management at both strategic and operational levels of action".

Drawing upon the literature on both public and private management, a common pattern can be discerned. Crises can be expected in both the routine and non-routine activities of an organisation. Among such studies, Fink (1986) presents four stages of a crisis. These include a warning stage, an acute crisis stage, a chronic crisis stage and crisis resolution. He also emphasises comprehensive crisis management plans, the compilation of critical information, and the flexibility of plans and fluidity of processes to allow the decision-maker adequate freedom to operate.

For administrative organisations, Rosenthal and Kouzmin (1997) suggest four key dimensions of government for managing crises. "First, the *administrative system* confronted with the threat: local, regional, national levels of government and even the transnational administrative structures involved need to be clarified. ... Second, the administrative *level* (local, regional, national, international) that eventually takes decisive action and controls the emergency response is important. The levels of government potentially involved in crisis response do not always coincide. .... Third, the dimension of the *speed* of government intervention --- which varies between the extremes of preemptive and delayed --- needs to be understood. Some crises are not immediately perceived by dominant governmental actors as needing government intervention --- Finally, the *scope* and strategy of government intervention --- closed versus open response modes --- need to be considered. A closed strategy entails a confined approach that minimizes the degree of external involvement, media attention, and public initiatives. In an open crisis, government takes the contrary position and actively encourages the mobilization of a variety of forces. .... More often than not, proactive media coverage or the sheer momentum of events results in active outside participation. Moreover, during different stages of a crisis, different actors and agencies may actually pursue different courses of action" (pp. 295-97).

The management of crises in public services must take cognisance of these dimensions. It is necessary to determine the level and degree of involvement and impact of the problem on various administrative organisations. While service areas are imprecisely separated, in many ways public organisations continue to be interdependent. This becomes more evident in crisis situations, when a number of actions have to be taken simultaneously by various agencies. The delivery of public services requires the performance of a core of activities by a designated agency, along with crucial support provided by others that may not be directly responsible. Hence, managing a crisis in the area of commerce, for example, entails actions not only by the relevant ministry/department, but also by agencies involved in managing information, public relations, finance, external relations and others who may be affected by the crisis or have a role to play in its dissipation.

Therefore, managing crises in public services calls for an overwhelming range of activities. Routine administrative activities have to be supplemented with arrangements to ensure constant vigilance for detecting signs of potential crises. Public managers must be able to identify a crisis event at its inception, and alert the core and other agencies to set in motion the process of management. Such action also calls for the adequate decentralisation of authority and the devolution of power, as well as a well co-ordinated plan of action. Along with such measures, public agencies need to keep the government and public informed of the nature of the problem, the extent of damage incurred or expected, and the options available to deal with the crisis. As the situation is brought under control, a continuous flow of information to the clients of services, the media and the public in general constitutes an invaluable element of managing crises in the public services.

Issues of Importance

Hong Kong's provision of public services has generally been commended for the quality and coverage. Over the years, various changes have been introduced in the political and organisational set-up, which may have an impact on their provision. The management of public services entails a number of routine and predictable activities, as well as numerous difficult, indeed nearly impossible tasks. Good management of public services should enable administrators to strike a balance among these dimensions of their work, and help society overcome a crisis with minimal damage. This study will draw upon the case studies to identify specific areas of strengths and weaknesses in the management of public services in Hong Kong, in order to provide a better understanding of its process in the post-handover period.

A number of questions will receive careful consideration. The provision of public services has evolved very slowly as the government of Hong Kong chose to adopt a 'hands-off' approach. The colonial nature of the government was reflected in its policy of providing a minimum level and range of services, while allowing market forces to determine price and coverage. The net effect has been a very healthy exchequer with continuous budget surpluses, as well as minimal expectation and demand from the public. Consequently, the quality and quantity of public services remained at a low level.

As Hong Kong underwent rapid economic development, concurrent changes took place in the social and political arena, and the government was compelled to rethink its strategies in providing public services. In view of the scheduled return of sovereignty to the People's Republic of China, a number of steps were undertaken during the 1980s and 1990s, many of which were aimed at extending and improving the methods and mechanisms of providing public services. Reforms introduced in the public sector in 1989 ushered in a series of measures for improving productivity, the delivery of public services and for enhancing their quality. Initial assessments suggested a reasonable degree of success (see Huque & Lee, 1996; Huque et.al., 1999), although it was argued that the reforms were motivated by political considerations (Cheung, 1992).

The reforms and new measures were set in motion while major changes were taking place in society and governmental arrangements. Political reforms at the fag end of British rule sought to take Hong Kong towards a completely representative system, while China raised strong objections to such a sudden acceleration of democratisation. The economy, after a prolonged period of continued growth, showed signs of slowing down. Citizens were ambivalent about the changes and the future of Hong

Kong, and a huge number of people left the territory to seek abode elsewhere. With the exodus of skilled manpower, public services were affected to some extent, but the reforms went ahead and various schemes were devised to attain their main objectives (see, for example, Efficiency Unit, 1995).

At the same time, various measures were undertaken to prepare the Civil Service for the transition. Training programmes were heavily oriented towards an inculcation of deeper knowledge about China and the development of language expertise among public servants (Huque & Lee, 1996). General views on the management of public services remained unchanged; although the preparatory measures during the run up to the transition did not seem to take into consideration the potential loss of expertise. Localisation became the order of the day, with expatriate officials at the highest levels gradually being replaced by locals (Lee & Huque, 1995). Preparation for 1997 concentrated on the acquisition of knowledge about China and language proficiency, while there seemed little emphasis on the possible loss of expertise and experience at the top level of the Civil Service.

The specific cases presented in this book intend to shed light on the management of public services with reference to public servants' level of preparedness, capability, and competence in dealing with crisis situations. Various questions come to mind with regard to the government's responsibility in explaining extraordinary steps taken to deal with critical issues. Does it have a responsibility to explain its personnel decisions to the public in the interest of transparency and public confidence? Are there crucial aspects of management that were neglected in dealing with the threat to public health? Is there a need for the government to be seen to be fair and impartial in dealing with corruption? Did the steps taken by the public agencies help or hinder the resolution of the problem?

It will be useful to assess the effectiveness of the management of public services in Hong Kong at this juncture of time. The problems may have been a consequence of past legacy, as under a colonial system of government public servants were inclined to keep the public at a distance. Such an approach appears to be unsuitable for the existing and changed circumstances. Alternatively, the problems may be attributed to the changes introduced in preparing Hong Kong as a Special Administrative Region of China. It could also simply be a matter of administrative inefficiency. The new political and administrative arrangements may have affected the capability to manage public services in Hong Kong. The problems could also be viewed as the result of bottlenecks in the process of communication between public organisations and the consumers of their services.

The specific cases will have to be examined in great detail, and ideas available in the general literature on public service management will be used to put information into perspective. The ultimate objective is to provide readers with a good understanding of the management of public services in Hong Kong, and inform them of recent developments to complete the picture.

First, the transition undergone by Hong Kong in the past three decades could have contributed to the problems. The territory has been under a constant state of flux due to the rapid economic and commercial development, and that resulted in a number of challenges. While a section of the population thrived on the freedom to pursue free enterprise in Hong Kong, this also expanded the number of people contributing to the process as hired workers. A regular flow of migrants from the mainland added to the pressure faced by the public services. However, through the general increase in the level of affluence, it was possible to provide a reasonable level of public services. The residents, for their part, were quite satisfied with the services provided, considering the fact that they were an improvement upon the previous arrangements. The government adopted a highly conservative strategy of expanding services at a slow pace. Even those such as basic education and health care took some time to be organised.

Before the territory could settle down into this comfortable mould of service provision, another issue of transition overwhelmed Hong Kong. The Joint Declaration, signed by the governments of the United Kingdom and Northern Ireland and the People's Republic of China in 1984, gave rise to concern and apprehension over the future of the territory and its position in the Chinese political system after the handover. Over the following 13 years, long and often bitter bargaining and negotiations continued between the two parties, in which the interests of Britain and China appeared to be uppermost in the minds of the two governments. Hong Kong and its people were not accorded their rightful place in the planning and charting of the future course of the territory. Consequently, such uncertainty about the future prompted a large number of residents to secure insurance through emigration and many left the territory. This was another aspect of the transition which had an impact on the management of public services, as several public officials chose to emigrate.

The somewhat haphazard response of the government to various events of a difficult nature could be related to this factor. As members of the public service grew increasingly apprehensive of the fate of Hong Kong following the return of sovereignty to China, many opted to collect their retirement benefits and seek a place of residence abroad, most commonly in Canada, Australia, the United Kingdom, the United States of America or New Zealand. Table I, below, shows the number of civil servants who took retirement or early retirement during this period. Such a large-scale exodus of experienced and efficient public servants may have affected the capability of the Civil Service.

Table I. Civil Service Retirement Statistics

	Normal Retirement		Voluntary Retirement		Total Retirement
	At 55	Over 55	Age 45-49	Age 50-54	
1984-85	447	289	139	188	1168
1985-86	410	276	163	188	1120
1986-87	330	191	131	164	900
1987-88	452	193	159	182	1072
1988-89	579	229	160	191	1259
1989-90	569	272	141	181	1272
1990-91	568	447	223	202	1926
1991-92	604	673	284	258	2267
1992-93	604	1150	330	253	2732
1993-94	685	952	337	248	3479
1994-95	686	955	494	380	3509
1995-96	464	1056	518	394	3982
1996-97	335	1246	459	606	4637
1997-98	255	828	463	701	3936

(Civil Service Personnel Statistics 1984 to Civil Service Personnel Statistics 1998, Civil Service Bureau Government Secretariat)

The problem may have been further exacerbated by stipulations laid down in *The Basic Law of the Hong Kong Special Administrative Region of the People's Republic of China*. Article 101 stipulates that "only Chinese citizens among permanent residents of the Region with no right of abode in any foreign country may fill the following posts: the Secretaries and deputy Secretaries of Departments, Directors of Bureaux, Commissioner Against Corruption, Director of Audit, Commissioner of Police, Director of Immigration and Commissioner of Customs and Excise". This provision had an impact on the career plans of a number of senior expatriate public officials, who had served Hong Kong for a long period of time. Many among this group chose to leave the service, while those who remained did so with the understanding that their role would be limited under the new circumstances. Consequently, Hong Kong may have lost more experienced and capable administrators, whose actions could have made a difference to the outcome of critical situations.

In addition to the uncertainties arising from transition and the departure of experienced administrators, the events may have reached crisis proportions due to a lack of effective communication between the government and the community. The new Chief Executive, in the first instance, was selected and appointed by the Central People's Government of China, and naturally was not dependent upon the mandate of the citizens of Hong Kong. The Basic Law allowed the Chief Executive to appoint his council of advisors or members of the Executive Council "from among the principal officials of the executive authorities, members of the Legislative Council and public figures", and their appointment and removal are "decided by the Chief Executive" (Article 55). This provision further weakened the link between the government and the public. Therefore, as Hong Kong faced a number of crises, there was no attempt by the government or its Civil Service to explain the problems faced or the alternative strategies for their resolution. Neither was any reassurance forthcoming for the assistance of the various parties affected by the threats to public confidence, public health or even the use of public facilities. Hence, the lack of an effective public relations mechanism in the new Hong Kong SAR government added to the perception that the administrators had been caught off-guard and had no clear idea of how to deal with the crises on their hands.

The Study

This book is expected to contribute to the bank of knowledge on public sector and crisis management in modern governments. It will be worthwhile to trace specific cases to chronicle the emergence of problems, their escalation into crises, the reaction and response of the public organisations and government to the events, and assess the results. The study will update and shed light on a number of interesting areas of public management, and point toward potential areas of crisis and their resolution. At present, there is no information available in a systematic form on these aspects of public services in Hong Kong.

The book contains six chapters. The first chapter will set the tone for a discussion of issues related to the management of public services, with reference to the available literature - both international and local. The objective is to determine the scope and method of study and set the agenda for research in a study of this nature. This will be followed by an analysis of the structural and procedural changes introduced for administering Hong Kong in recent times, and an attempt to determine the nature of the relationships among the public services, the Chief Executive and the Legislative Council.

The following four chapters will each deal with a case of crisis faced by the Hong Kong public service, both immediately before and after the handover in July 1997. Each case study will provide detailed information on a specific case, followed by an analysis based on the framework established in the first chapter. Chapter Two explores the issue of management of personnel matters at the highest level, while Chapter Three considers the management of an unexpected crisis in the form of avian flu. Chapter Four sheds light on the complex issue of public confidence in the legal system in the SAR, and Chapter Five examines the problems related to the opening of Hong Kong's most expensive and huge public transport infrastructure, Hong Kong International Airport. Following the analyses related to specific cases, Chapter Six provides an assessment of the role of the Civil Service in managing public services and anticipating and responding to major crises. This should be useful in understanding the nature of operation of this vital institution in Hong Kong's new environment, and will assist in developing insight into the process of local public service management.

2 Managing Public Interest

Public interest has long been an issue of debate in the social sciences. Not only is it difficult to define "public interest" in precise terms, but it may be perceived differently depending on the people involved. Generally, an act "is said to be in the *public interest* if it serves the ends of the whole public rather than those of some sector of the public" (Banfield, 1977: 44). One of the distinguishing features of governmental obligation is the promotion of public interest, which can be considered as a general guide for public officials' actions (Rosenbloom, 1989: 8). There are several methods and mechanisms in modern states for ensuring public interest, and the use of legislative surveillance and citizen participation have been recommended for this purpose (see Henry, 1995: 390).

Downs, however, sounds a note of caution with regard to the private and public motives of officials. "Although many officials serve the public interest as they perceive it, it does not necessarily follow that they are privately motivated solely or even mainly by a desire to serve the public interest *per se*. ... Society cannot insure that it will be served merely by assigning someone to serve it" (Downs, 1967: 87).

The confusion over what constitutes public interest may contribute to the power of bureaucracy in a country, and could result in unilateral decisions on their part. In the absence of effective institutions to monitor the operation of the bureaucracy, officials often use the promotion of public interest as a rationalisation of their decisions and actions. In such cases, public interest is cited as the cause of particular actions, and any attempt to question such decisions is summarily rejected.

The resignation of the Director of Immigration in Hong Kong in 1996 is a case in point. A process of political development had been set in motion since the early 1990s, and the strength and role of the legislature had been gradually enhanced. The level of citizens' participation in public affairs was also on the rise in the new environment, under which there was heightened expectation about the responsive and transparent nature of the public service. However, the government sought to define public interest unilaterally and claimed that the decision to allow the Director of Immigration to retire after an exceedingly short notice was justified in the

23

public interest. The community had no hesitation in challenging such a claim.

The Case

On 6th July 1996, the Secretary for the Civil Service, Lam Woon-kwong, announced that after considering the "special personal situation" of the Director of Immigration, Laurence Leung Ming-yin, his application for retirement was approved and the regular 12 month pre-retirement notice waived. This allowed Leung to be immediately relieved of his duties. Further details of Leung's private reasons for resignation were undisclosed, however, on the grounds that the government had an obligation to keep employees' personal information confidential.

The government spared no effort to keep the issue under wraps. The argument was simple: it was the government's duty to respect Leung's right to privacy. "We [the government] respect [Leung's] personal wish. We won't make public the reason for his retirement", asserted Donald Tsang Yam-kuen, acting Governor at the time (*South China Morning Post*, 13th July 1996). The Secretary for the Civil Service insisted professional conduct to safeguard personal information prevented him from revealing Leung's private reasons for departure (*Minutes of Special Legco Panel on Public Service*, Para. 8). Other government officials maintained that any break from the code of confidentiality before the handover would discredit the government as an employer, diminish Civil Service morale and ultimately affect Hong Kong's political stability (Hon & Yeung, *South China Morning Post*, 12th July 1996).

Public Intrigue and Concern

The public was outraged by the announcement. The Director of Immigration was a key negotiator in the Sino-British Joint Liaison Group (JLG), which was charged with the task of leading an expert committee in the consideration of the Special Administrative Region's passport and the status of permanent residents. If these two issues were not resolved within the year, they would have a serious impact upon people travelling to and from Hong Kong, and could ultimately adversely affect the economy. Thus, allowing Leung to leave so hurriedly, in the course of fulfilling his duties, seemed imprudent and almost reckless. The stipulated twelve month pre-retirement period, prescribed by the *Civil Service Regulations 327(5)*, was designed primarily to prevent such a scenario. It was expected to help ensure a stable and predictable bureaucratic structure, and to allow time to identify an appropriate successor to whom responsibilities could be transferred. Yet, according to official reports, Leung departed from his office within a few days of submitting his application, and there were rumours that he left within hours. Permitting a senior civil servant to leave at such short notice was unprecedented. Clearly, there was an urgent need for Leung to vacate his post immediately, and because the government created an air of mystery around the case by not providing any explanation for the resignation, concern and speculation abound.

The media was quick to sense the potential for public interest in the case and soon a large number of journalists were investigating Leung's private life. He had good relations with Pro-Beijing businessmen and Chinese officials, making it easy to invent theories behind his resignation, fueling public hunger for any explanation for the event. Rumours spread that Leung, being a foreign passport holder and subsequently unable to retain his position in the post-handover Civil Service as a directorate-grade officer, had been recruited by a prominent pro-China figure (Kwang, *Straits Times*, 10th July 1996; *South China Morning Post*, 8th July 1996). A number of British newspapers reported that Leung's departure was related to possible breaches of confidentiality of information entrusted to him as Director of Immigration (*Select Committee Report*, Vol.1, Para. 4.1 and 4.2).

Objections to the Government's Evasiveness

Meanwhile, government evasiveness became a subject of debate between key public figures. Legislators were concerned that the secrecy was the result of a contravention of public interest. Legislator Leong Che-hung raised the issue in his weekly column in the *Hong Kong Standard*, "[a]ny public figure or high ranking civil servant will come under public scrutiny and any irregularities in their movement must be an issue of public interest. Legislators, as elected representatives of the public are duty bound to ensure the reasons behind his resignation are identified and that the public interest is not jeopardized" (*Hong Kong Standard*, 20th July 1996).

A legal expert at the University of Hong Kong raised the issue of government accountability. "It has been argued that there ought not to be any further invasions of Mr. Leung's privacy. But, Mr. Leung was not a private citizen employed by a private firm on private terms of service. He was a senior civil servant, holding a very important and sensitive office in the public service and paid from public funds. The community has a right to expect the government to make a full and true disclosure of all the facts and circumstances leading to this most unusual termination of service" (Jayawickrama, *Hong Kong Standard,* 17th July 1996).

Another legislator, Cheung Man-kwong, expressed suspicion of a cover-up. "Mr. Patten has pledged that there is no secret agenda under his rule. However, both the Legislative Council and the Executive Council do not know the true story behind Mr. Leung's sudden retirement while only the top echelon of the Government knows what is going on. Clearly this is a secret agenda. Chris Patten should be held responsible for not keeping his promise" (*South China Morning Post*, 15th July 1996).

The media was quick to lend support to this line of criticism. For years, Patten and his officers boasted of transparency and accountability while criticising the closed-door policy of the Chinese regime. In view of the Leung case, the government's performance was reminiscent of when governmental transparency was not much better than that of the highly-secretive Chinese administration. Yet, with this case, even top Chinese Officials who closely watched Hong Kong's local affairs demanded an explanation. Director of the Hong Kong and Macau Affairs Office, Lu Ping, complained that, "...Mr. Leung just packed his things and went home...This is not normal. It came suddenly. But the government still has to explain clearly why Mr. Leung left - not only to China, but also to the Hong Kong public" (No & Li, *South China Morning Post,* 11th July 1996).

Leung's Explanation

As speculation ran rife, Leung finally emerged from his home on the evening of 9th July 1996 to explain the cause of his sudden resignation. "Since my daughter's death, it's been psychologically draining. Work pressure has been very great...I have no plans to join any private company. In short, I have no plans to do anything at all, just recover my health. I have no foreign passport. I have a BNO [British National (Overseas)] passport and after 1997 I will remain in Hong Kong" (Lo, Hong & Wong, *South China Morning Post,* 10th July 1996).

The public was expecting an explanation that would dispel rumours and put an end to speculation, and was disappointed with the statement. It was well known that Leung's daughter, Sylvia, was murdered at the British Columbia Institute of Technology in Vancouver, Canada by the bolt of a powerful crossbow (Szeto, *South China Morning Post,* 24th January 1997).

However, after three years, it did not seem to be an adequate reason for such a sudden retirement.

Government Irritation at Repeated Demands for an Explanation

The Governor and his officials were becoming increasingly irritated by the attention the matter had gained. They were particularly annoyed that the public would challenge the privilege traditionally enjoyed by the government and not accept their final word on the case. From Europe, Governor Chris Patten firmly reasserted the government's stance: "Mr. Leung retired for personal reasons and as far as I am concerned, personal reasons are personal reasons" (Lo, Hon & Wong, *South China Morning Post,* 10th July 1996). The acting Governor, Donald Tsang, was even more blunt. He accused the media of sensationalising the case, invading Leung's privacy and aggravating public anxieties. "Public interest has been enlarged to the extent that [it] includes the curiosity of anyone to know something about other people…it's been abused" (Yeung, *South China Morning Post,* 17th July 1996). Tsang rejected the suggestion that there was collective deceit on the part of the government and demanded that they should be able to keep some issues secret.

Such a response outraged the media. The *South China Morning Post* published a powerful editorial criticising the acting Governor for his comments: "[Donald Tsang's] attack on media coverage…reveals an alarming intolerance that calls into question the sincerity of the government's repeated pledges of press freedom. Instead of recognizing the serious public concern aroused by the overnight departure of a civil servant occupying one of the most sensitive posts in the administration, Mr. Tsang opted for the far easier expedient of accusing the media of creating the whole controversy. He claimed the press had abused the notion of public interest: implying the community has no right to know anything the Government does not want to tell it" (*South China Morning Post,* 17th July 1996).

On 11th July 1996, the Secretary for the Civil Service, Lam Woon-kwong, was summoned to attend a special Legislative Council Public Services Panel meeting to discuss Leung's sudden departure. At the meeting, legislators expressed concern over the secrecy surrounding the case, which they claimed heightened speculation of a cover-up and undermined government credibility. They argued that public interest was at stake and as a result it was the right of the public to be informed of circumstances leading to Leung's immediate departure.

Lam went into details of legally prescribed retirement procedures outlined in the *Civil Service Regulations 327(5)* (CSR) and the government's careful use of discretion and regard for public interest in the handling of the case. He refuted the rumours that the government had incited Leung's retirement, explaining: "…Mr. Leung had a right to retire [he had reached the retirement age of 55 years] and he had chosen to retire on his own will. The administration had no power to ask for his retirement or to approve or disapprove of his retirement. The administration only had the authority to waive or shorten a notice period" (*Minutes of Panel Meeting*, Para. 4).

The Secretary for the Civil Service admitted that there could be public misgivings over the propriety of the waiver granted to Leung. But he assured that the government had exercised its authority with discretion and with due regard to public interest. The foremost concern at the time of the retirement, explained Lam, was whether there would be a succession problem and whether the efficiency of the Immigration Department would be affected by Leung's departure (*Minutes of panel meeting*, Para. 7). Lam told the Legislative Council that a qualified successor had been identified and the work of the Immigration Department had been running smoothly since the announcement, indicating no particular impact on public interest.

In Lam's opinion, there was really no reason to be worried about the Leung case. He felt that concern had been provoked by the nosiness of the media, which was similar to the interest the public has for the private lives of movie stars. He mocked legislators for their curiosity: "I'm concerned about many things. Who is [Taiwanese Movie star] Lin Ching-hsia married to and why someone in Shanghai said [Miss Hong Kong] Lee San-san is ugly. But that does not mean I have to ask Lee San-san to tell me why other people said she is ugly" (*Report of the Select Committee*, Vol. 1, Para. 5.35(f)). Such frivolous comments reflected the irritation, as well as the lack of preparation on the part of the Secretary for the Civil Service, to deal with the new environment of public management in Hong Kong.

The Chairman of the Public Services Panel concluded the meeting with the remark that Lam had been unable to clear the doubts attached to the matter of Leung's retirement and did not provide a satisfactory explanation. The tension between legislators and the administration mounted as the former requested legal advice for setting up a mechanism for conducting public inquiry into the case.

The Governor, Chris Patten, professed great indignation at the questions raised by the Legislative Council regarding the government's judgement. He immediately shot back at legislators saying that he would definitely not recall the Legislative Council during summer recess merely for the sake of holding a public inquiry into the case, and that "[he doesn't] think one should get these things out of proportion." (Yeung, *South China Morning Post,* 16th July 1996). The relationship between the administration and the Legislative Council was inherently averse.

The Governor's statement seemed to assert the fact that the Civil Service was instituted as a power beyond reproach, while the Legislative Council was the incoherent opposition. Both sides claimed to be the defender of public interest, but took completely different approaches for arriving at their conclusion of its essence. The relationship between the two branches of government had been improving over the years. However, the Civil Service retained its position as a privileged institution, while the Legislative Council had matured and strengthened its position as the legitimate representative of the public. The Leung case highlighted this tension and added to the strain in their interaction.

At a Special House Committee Meeting on 20th September 1996, the Public Service Panel reported its concern that the public may have been deprived of knowledge of an important issue where public interest might have been compromised. It therefore proposed an inquiry into the case, either by itself or a select committee (*House Committee Minutes,* 20th September 1996). After some discussion, members came to the consensus that a select committee would provide more flexibility and provide interested members outside the Public Services Panel an opportunity to participate in the process.

On 23rd October, Legislative Councillor Ip Kwok-him moved the following motion to set up the Select Committee:

> That a select committee be appointed to inquire into the circumstances surrounding the departure of Mr. Leung Ming-yin, former Director of Immigration, from the government and related issues; and that in the performance of its duties the committee be authorized under section 9(2) of the Legislative Council (Powers and Privileges) Ordinance (Cap. 382) to exercise the powers conferred by section 9(1) of that ordinance (*Legislative Council Minutes*, 23rd October 1996).

The Secretary for the Civil Service, in objection to the resolution stated:

> As a liberal and responsible government, we have all along been seeking to enhance the transparency of the Government. We also recognize that the

public has the right to know about public policies and administration. However, the right to know should not be extended indefinitely. As an employer, the Government must keep confidential the personal particulars and data of civil servants so long as public interests are not jeopardized, I repeat so long as public interests are not jeopardized and this case should be no exception (*Legislative Council Minutes*, 23rd October 1996).

The Select Committee consisted of 11 members of the Legislative Council: Ip Kwok-him (Chairman), Selina Chow, Ronald Arculli, Cheung Man-kwong, James To, Christine Loh, Law Cheung-kwok, Margaret Ng, Elizabeth Wong, Lawrence Yum and Philip Wong. They met for the first time on 8th November 1996 to determine the direction of their investigation. Philip Wong did not believe any of the Civil Service witnesses would reveal anything substantial (Braude, *South China Morning Post*, 5th January 1997). A few days later, it appeared as if Wong was right. After hearing the testimonies of seven civil servants, members were becoming frustrated at the minimal progress of the investigation.

Sudden Turn of Events: Leung's Testimony

On 10th January 1997, the Select Committee investigation took a surprising turn of events. Mr. Leung testified at the meeting with the following prepared statement:

> The death of my daughter in 1993 was a great blow to me. I thought of retiring, but then I considered it thoroughly and thought I should stay in my post, because in the transitional period, I had to settle a lot of immigration matters related to the general public.
>
> I have worked in the Immigration Department for more than 30 years. I must have made some contribution to the stability of Hong Kong. I have carried out my responsibilities and [decided I] should not quit because of what happened to me. So I decided to continue to work. However, my work in the three years after that involved a lot of man-made stumbling blocks, and there were a lot of picky queries about my work. At the time, I treated this as a test of myself. I insisted on not involving politics in my work and carried out my work with the interests of Hong Kong people at the forefront of my mind.
>
> In the morning of Sunday, October 1, 1995, more than 10 officers from the Independent Commission Against Corruption went to my office and my home to seize documents and bank passbooks and ornaments. They said the income earned by me for my post was not comparable to my wealth. It was demanded I explain.

During the investigation, I and my family suffered mental stress - but we kept calm. I thought I had done nothing wrong, and would never take personal benefits from my work. Most of my property was left to me by my mother. She divided her properties evenly into eight portions a few years before her death. I have submitted a lot of information on my economic situation.

After more than six months of investigation, the ICAC found out that I was innocent. They sent me a letter in April 1996 telling me this and apologizing to me for causing a disturbance. After that, I thought there was still fairness in the world. A righteous man should be treated fairly.

On July 4, 1996, I was asked to have a meeting with the Secretary for Civil Service Lam Woon-kwong at 10am on July 5, 1996, and I was asked [at the meeting] to submit a letter of retirement before 5pm the same day. Otherwise the Government would force me to retire.

I asked him the reason. He only said that the Government no longer trusted me. I asked the reason again. He said I should know the reason. I said I didn't know. I still do not.

Angry and sad I asked how my retirement should be explained to the public and the Immigration Department and what the arrangement would be for my successor and my work.

Mr. Lam said the Government would take care of it and it was not my business. I had just half a day to consider the case. Finally I decided to accept it.

I worked [for the Government] for 30 years and spared no effort in the performance of my duty. In return, I had been unreasonably sacked. I was shocked, embarrassed, disappointed and lost all hope. If I opposed what was being forced on me by the Government, there would be a great impact on society, and the morale of my department would be affected. I have to look at the overall situation.

Over the more than 30 years, I developed deep affection for the department. Its work has reached world standards of which I felt proud. I did not want my affairs to affect the attitude of my staff. I considered that I couldn't oppose the Government on my own. That would be like throwing eggs at rocks. As to why I decided to disclose these facts to legislators: there have been organized efforts to ruin my reputation. An example was that there were reports in the British media that I decided to increase the quota of one-way permits granted to Mainland Chinese; I sold confidential information and intelligence; and I allowed a Chinese organization to be responsible for printing Special Administrative Region passports in return for some benefits. I have to clarify that the decision [to increase the one-way permit quota] could not be made by me alone. It has to be passed by the Executive Council. It was a collective decision. The information in the Immigration Department is subject to strict security measures. Anyone, including the director, accessing the information is recorded by the computer. You can find out when exactly, which year, month, day, minute and second, anyone has retrieved information. The printing of the SAR passports is entirely a matter for the Chinese Government. It has nothing to do with the Hong Kong Government. I was just a little civil servant and did not have the power to question it.

I could tolerate losing my job, but I couldn't tolerate the accusations and not make objections. There will still be groundless accusations made against me. I was stuck without options and had to tell the truth to the council. The conclusion of the letter from the ICAC dated April 24, 1996 said: 'The investigation is over and a report submitted to the committee [ICAC Operations Review Committee]. We agreed with the report that the complaint made to us was without grounds and that the ICAC should not continue to investigate. The Commissioner of the ICAC has accepted the instructions. We were ordered to tell you this and apologize to you for the inconvenience caused (*South China Morning Post*, 11 January 1997).

The long statement issued by Leung underlined a breakdown of communication, not only between the government and the public, but also with public servants. This highlights an often-neglected aspect of public service management, in which mutual trust and understanding emerge as vital elements in the production, delivery and continuation of public services.

Government Retaliation

Leung's lengthy statement obviously touched a nerve in the government, and senior officials were quick to retaliate. A public statement was immediately released to explain the position of the government and the Secretary for the Civil Service on the issue:

The retirement of former Director of Immigration Laurence Leung is an employment matter between the Hong Kong Government and Mr. Leung himself. I want to state that the UK Government was not involved in the matter in any way. I have made it clear in my evidence to the Legco Select Committee that when I meet an officer to discuss their personal career situation, what passes between us remains confidential and should not be disclosed to third parties without the officer's consent.

Now that Mr. Leung has revealed the substance of my meeting with him on July 5, he has clearly waived the implied confidentiality of the meeting in question.

I can confirm that I invited him to the meeting on July 5. At the meeting, I told Mr. Leung that I was considering making a representation to the Governor under Colonial Regulation 59 that his retirement would be desirable in the public interest. But he could if he chose to, retire voluntarily with immediate effect.

Under Colonial Regulation 59, before a report is made to the Governor, an officer must be informed of the grounds on which his retirement is contemplated and would have been given the opportunity to make representation. The reports and any representation made by Mr. Leung would then have been submitted to the Governor for a decision whether, having regard to all the circumstances, the officer should be required to retire.

It was Mr. Leung's choice to retire rather than to face Colonial Regulation 59 action.

Mr. Leung volunteered to reveal today that he was the subject of an ICAC investigation and you will have seen a statement from the ICAC confirming that this was the case. I must explain again that in the absence of that disclosure by Mr. Leung and confirmation by the ICAC, I could not properly confirm or deny whether Mr. Leung had been the subject of an investigation.

I can further confirm that a copy of the ICAC's report was forwarded to the administration to consider whether any disciplinary or administrative action against Mr. Leung was necessary. I will now have to consider the transcript of Mr. Leung's evidence very carefully, in particular, his points about further disclosure of information. When we have done so, we will then consider whether we have anything more to say (*South China Morning Post*, 11th January 1997).

Over the next few days, the government employed intensive effort to defend the manner in which the case was handled. In the process, it was repeatedly emphasised that there had been no concealment or lies in the details provided about Leung's retirement. Financial Secretary Donald Tsang (who was the acting Governor during the announcement of Leung's retirement), Governor Chris Patten and Chief Secretary Anson Chan all supported the way in which the Secretary for the Civil Service managed the situation. Tsang stated that "Mr. Lam handled the issue with 'justice and consideration', taking into account the public interest, Mr. Leung's long service and personal feelings" (Chan & Tsui, *South China Morning Post*, 12th January 1997).

The Chief Secretary, Anson Chan, made a statement on 22nd January to further clarify the situation and defend the position taken by the Civil Service and the government of Hong Kong:

I wish to make it clear that the Administration has not lied nor sought to mislead this Committee. All officers appearing before Members [of the Committee] have tried to answer questions put to them as honestly as they could bearing in mind the limitations imposed by the rule of confidentiality. As the Secretary for the Civil Service, Mr. WK Lam, has made clear, it is an unwritten rule well understood by all civil servants that matters discussed between an officer and the Secretary for the Civil Service concerning personal and employment matters should remain confidential and should not be divulged publicly unless and until the officer concerned consents to disclosure. Strict adherence to this rule is crucial for the good management of the Civil Service. Mr. Lam gave his word to Mr. Leung that he would regard Mr. Leung's retirement as a personal matter between him and the Government. Mr. Lam was simply not in a position to give this Committee as comprehensive a response as you would have liked. I hope you will make allowance for the constraints facing Mr. Lam and other officers who were summoned before this Committee (Legislative Council, *Report*, Volume 2, SE.E/019 Para.2).

First Success of the Select Committee

Meanwhile, the public, along with legislators, appeared to be happy with the triumph of the Powers and Privileges Ordinance. This Ordinance authorises the Legislative Council to summon witnesses to present evidence in the form of testimony or documentation before the Council or a select committee. The refusal to give evidence can be allowed if it could be proved that it would not affect the subject or procedure of inquiry. However, if the claim cannot be substantiated, Section 26 of the Ordinance permits prosecution with the consent of the Attorney General. Section 14 provides for exceptions whereby a testimony or documentation may be waived if it concerns any military matter relating to the security of Hong Kong; responsibilities other than those in respect to the administration of Hong Kong by its government; and secondary evidence.

In Defence of the Government

On 15th January, 1997, the Secretary for the Civil Service arrived at the televised Select Committee meeting, armed with the draft letter that would have been sent to Leung if he would have chosen to face charges brought against him under CR59. The draft letter listed four reasons, based on findings from the ICAC report, behind government suspicions:

First, it was pointed out that Mr. Leung had obtained a loan of $1.76 million from the Government in February 1989 under the Housing Loan Scheme to purchase a property in Canada. He subsequently sold the property in 1991 but failed to report the sale to the Civil Service Branch as required under Paragraph 6 of the Terms and Conditions of the Housing Loan Scheme.

Secondly, in response to a letter dated 3 May 1995 from the Secretary for Security requiring him to declare his investments, Mr. Leung failed to disclose the full details of his investments, namely his interests in Macrun Profits Ltd, Dragon House Investment Ltd and Fortune Score Ltd.

Thirdly, Mr. Leung had entered into business relations [Dragon House Investment Ltd] with Hon. Lau Wong fat, a Legislative Council Member, but had failed to disclose such details of such relations to the Secretary for Security.

Fourthly...since becoming Director of Immigration, he had invested $100,000 in a company called New Hong Kong China Advertising Limited with a view to developing advertising business in Mainland China. Notwithstanding the fact that the company was subsequently wound up due to its failure to obtain a business license in Mainland China, the Government considered it unacceptable that an officer of Mr. Leung's seniority and position should seek to start a business venture in mainland China, as he did, without reporting the full details of such a business venture to the Secretary for Security (Legislative Council, *Report*, Volume 2, Summary of Section B of Chapter 2: Reasons for Contemplating Action under Colonial Regulation 59).

The Secretary for the Civil Service also admitted the existence of an integrity report, confirming misgivings towards Leung. "Integrity checks are a different thing. It will only be given to the Civil Service Branch for consideration....It's not related to the ICAC report. We do them regularly. It's a coincidence that it's completed at that time. We have considered the report in assessing the integrity of Mr. Leung ... the conclusion of the integrity report confirms the impression of Leung in the ICAC report" (*South China Morning Post*, 16th January 1997). Yet, he added that "[t]hese reports, if existing, are related to the security, confidential matters, and are exempted [from disclosure] because of public interest... The integrity check is a thorough and detailed one...built on trust and confidentiality. It cannot be published in a casual way. It involves many persons and matters" (*South China Morning Post*, 16th January 1997).

Public Views on Government Action against Leung

Despite the new revelations made by the government, legislators echoed the opinion of the public and questioned the appropriateness of Leung's retirement. "If [those four reasons stated by the government] were the real reasons the government did not need to terminate Mr. Leung's duties immediately", said Legislator Cheng Yiu-tong. Liberal Party Legislator, Allen Lee Peng-fei and Democratic Party Legislator, Yeung Sum, shared similar doubts that the reasons for Leung's serious punishment could be as simple as that stated by the government. "The four reasons given by Mr. Lam were simply related to the economic interests of Mr. Leung. There may be more complex reasons behind (the forced retirement)", said Yeung (So, *HKSTD*, 16th January 1997).

Lam responded to public conjecture on the issue by calling it "the most appropriate action" (*South China Morning Post*, 16th January 1997). "He [Leung] chose to hide [the details of his breaches]…as head of the Civil Service branch, I am greatly disappointed in him. Personally, I am disgusted with this behavior. If he has no guilty conscience, he did not have to choose to retire" (Yeung & Hon, *South China Morning Post*, 16th January 1997). Governor Chris Patten said he was "utterly amazed" at claims that Leung's breaches were "minor matters" and he "should have been slapped on the wrist and allowed to continue". Patten opined that Leung's behaviour had fallen "well below--- well below---the standard of confidence and integrity we rightly expect of our public service" (Yeung & No, *South China Morning Post*, 17th January 1997).

Following this tone of the government's argument, the Chief Secretary attempted to emphasise the severity of the charges in a statement issued on 22nd January 1997:

> It has been suggested by some that non-disclosure of assets and investments and failure to repay a housing loan were mere indiscretions or technical breaches, not sufficiently serious to warrant instant dismissal or forced retirement.
>
> As head of the Civil Service, I have to say that I disagree strongly. Mr. Leung has blatantly disregarded rules, despite having his attention drawn specifically to the requirements and warned of the consequences of non-compliance, that is disciplinary action or dismissal. Mr. Leung headed an important disciplinary force responsible for a range of sensitive issues that could affect every man, woman and child in Hong Kong as well as overseas visitors.   On his leadership depended the reputation of the entire Immigration Department, not only in the eyes of the local community, but also with overseas Governments.

In the course of his normal duties, Mr. Leung himself would have taken disciplinary action against junior officers for similar or other breaches. Rules governing conduct and discipline apply equally to both junior and senior staff. Indeed we take a more serious view of breaches by senior staff from whom we demand a high standard of personal integrity, absolute honesty and accountable behavior. The community would expect no less.

In our view, each of the offenses listed in the letter which would have been sent to Mr. Leung was sufficiently serious on its own to warrant action. Taken together, they cast serious doubt over Mr. Leung's integrity, character and his suitability to remain in post.

We decided that Mr. Leung must leave the service quickly. Our concern was to minimize adverse impact on staff morale, and to avoid tarnishing the image of the Immigration Department which could in turn have undermined the confidence which other countries have in our immigration services. It was Mr. Leung's choice to retire immediately (as he was perfectly entitled to do). If Mr. Leung had chosen to face action under CR59, he would have been interdicted from duty immediately. There could be no question of his remaining in post whilst facing CR59 proceedings. Equally, it would have been imprudent to allow Mr. Leung to remain in charge of sensitive issues and systems whilst serving his period of notice, however short, given the circumstances of his departure. In this instance, it is entirely reasonable for us to require Mr. Leung to leave his post with one day's notice. Indeed in the private sector, little notice is given in similar circumstances (Legislative Council, *Report*, Volume 2, SE/E/019 Para. 4).

Powers and Privileges of the Legislative Councillors

On 17th January, the Governor called an urgent breakfast meeting with the policy secretaries. He wanted to discuss the demand made by the Select Committee the previous day for the disclosure of the integrity report and the ICAC's Operations Review Committee Report on Leung. The chairman of the Select Committee cautioned that legal action for contempt would be taken if the Chief Secretary Anson Chan appeared before the Select Committee on Wednesday, 22nd January without copies of the reports.

On 22nd January, with the concurrence of the Select Committee, the Chief Secretary and the Secretary for the Civil Service produced, in camera, a summary of the integrity report. Confidentiality was assured under the premise that the full disclosure of the report would put the integrity checking system at risk, and this would subsequently deprive the government of a valuable means for assessing the credibility of senior civil servants. The Deputy Commissioner of the Police confirmed that the summary contained all the essential information considered for the conclusion. Edited videotapes of ICAC interviews with Leung were also produced. Yet, the actual Operations Review Committee Report (ORC Report) was withheld. The Chief Secretary, in a letter to the Chairman of the Select Committee, explained her reasons:

> Having taken the advice of the Commissioner [of ICAC], (who in turn has taken advice of the ORC itself) I am of the opinion that to disclose a copy of the ORC Report itself even in camera would compromise the future operations of the ORC.
>
> The ICAC operates on the basic principle of confidentiality. If confidentiality cannot be assured, sources may be inhibited from providing information to the ICAC which would have an adverse effect on investigations. Reports prepared for the ORC contain full details for investigation, together with comments, views and assessment including legal advice, by the professional concerned. The information is provided to the ORC on a mutual trust basis. Any release of the information to third parties would undermine that trust and consequentially the effectiveness of the ORC in its monitoring role. Neither the ICAC nor the ORC could operate effectively if ORC Reports were to be given to third parties (Legislative Council, *Report*, Volume 2, SE/E/030).

The Select Committee found the reasons provided by the Chief Secretary unjustifiable, but decided that the issue would not be pressed any further should the Chairman be given access to the ORC report. The Chairman could then advise the Committee on its contents. However, this option was rejected by the administration. The Committee again summoned the Chief Secretary to appear with a copy of the ORC report. Days later, the Committee received an Originated Summons issued by the Attorney General, claiming the Chief Secretary may be exempted from producing the ORC report, and this sparked off a debate over the possible conflict of interest with regard to the relationship between the Attorney General and the Chief Secretary. It was obvious that the former would side with the latter in this issue of major controversy.

At the hearing on 24th April, the Chief Secretary read out a statement to the Select Committee reiterating her reasons for non-disclosure of the report as previously stated in her letter to the Chairman. She also distributed a 'Certificate of Chief Secretary' to legislators repeating the same claims, before entering into private chambers to further discuss with the Chairman, in confidence, the reasons for her refusal to produce the ORC report. The Chairman adjourned the meeting to take legal advice and resumed hearings on 9th May to deliver his opinion:

At the hearing on 24 April 1997, after making a formal claim of privilege the Chief Secretary decided to explain her reasons in confidence to me. Her reasons were no more than what she had already said to the Committee. What she made clear was that she was not prepared to produce the Report to me as Chairman of the Committee under the Resolution procedures.

In all the circumstances, it is my opinion that the Chief Secretary has not provided sufficient reason to justify her claim of privilege on the ground that the production of the ORC Report would be contrary to the public interest (Legislative Council, *Report*, Volume 1, Appendix V).

Following the delivery of the Chairman's opinion, the Select Committee again advised the Chief Secretary to produce a copy of the ORC report to the Chairman, allowing her to delete the names of persons and comments, views and assessment, including legal advice, of the professionals concerned. On 15th May the Chief Secretary, "with some misgivings", surrendered an edited version of the ORC Report to the Chairman.

The Executive-Legislative Rift

The Select Committee could not proceed much further due to the lack of co-operation from the government and the central secretariat. On 19th May 1997, after viewing the evidence, the Chairman issued a statement:

> After perusing the ICAC Report to the Operations Review Committee…I am of the view that the ORC Report contains no material information upon which the Government's decision was ultimately based which had been omitted from the information supplied to the Committee. I have reported my conclusion to the Select Committee.
>
> The Committee deeply regrets that the Chief Secretary, instead of cooperating with the Committee to find ways acceptable to both the Committee and the Government for producing the ORC Report, has resorted to instituting court proceedings before the Chairman of the Committee has formed an opinion as to whether her claim for public interest immunity is valid pursuant to the Resolution of the Legislative Council made and passed under Section 15 of the Legislative Council (Powers and Privileges) Ordinance (Legislative Council, *Report*, Volume 1, Appendix VI).

On the same day, the Attorney General discontinued legal proceedings to grant exemption to the Chief Secretary from producing the ORC report to the Select Committee.

On 11th June the Select Committee released its final report. Interestingly, the report approved the government's decision to immediately release Leung. At the same time, the Committee condemned the manner in which the government chose to execute its decision. The report read:

> The seniority and sensitivity of Mr. Leung's position give all the more reason for demanding from him exemplary honesty and integrity... members consider that each of the four incidents cited in the Secretary for Civil Service's draft letter is on its own of a serious nature and warrants consideration of disciplinary action... In the light of the evidence that Mr. Leung had breached the Civil Service Regulations...the majority of the Committee consider it understandable and reasonable for the Government to doubt the character and integrity of Mr. Leung.
>
> [However] in the Committee's view, an open and fair Government should have given Mr. Leung a full account of the grounds for its proposed actions when notifying him of its decision to require him to leave the service... the Committee deeply regrets that...Government officials had tailored their evidence and consciously withheld material information in the attempt to mislead the Legislative Council and the public into accepting an account of Mr. Leung's departure from government service, which they know to be untrue.
>
> The Committee finds the remarks of the Secretary for Civil Service unacceptable not only because they were misleading, but also because they reflected a frivolous attitude in response to the proper concern of the Legislative Council and the public.
>
> The Committee accepts that the Government's motive was out of public interest reasons, and not for the purpose of concealing misconduct. Nevertheless, the Government's duty to be accountable to the Legislative Council and the community at large for its policies and actions is paramount (Legislative Council, *Report*, Volume 2, Chapter 5).

Thus, the need for the government to be accountable and transparent was highlighted. Days later, on 18th June 1997, the Legislative Council passed a motion endorsing the Select Committee Report. In his speech, the Chairman of the Committee remarked:

> ...[G]overnment officials have time and again challenged the source of power of the Select Committee, as well as questioned the powers we have. The uncooperative attitude of the government officials has no doubt reflected that the Government did have the intention to obstruct the Select Committee from exercising its proper powers. ...[I]nstead of cooperating

sincerely with the Select Committee, the Government has all along 'tailored' efforts to frustrate the Select Committee's investigation work. One cannot but remain in doubt as to why the Government has chosen to respond in such a way which not only brought it into disrepute and undermined its credibility...

...[T]he Government could explain with appropriate reasons its refusal to disclose the information regarding decisions that should be kept confidential, it should never seek to intentionally mislead the Legislative Council and the community at large or conceal the truth by telling lies or giving untrue answers and still making serious claims that it has already disclosed everything. This is unacceptable to us.

...[T]his inquiry has rendered the Select Committee rather helpless in the pretext of public interests. As such, not every part of the proceedings involved in this inquiry has been disclosed to the public. It is for these reasons that the Select Committee cannot give the public a full account of the case or disclose everything involved. In my opinion, this is most regrettable" (*Legislative Council Minutes*, 18th June 1997).

The case appeared to be heading towards a predictable conclusion. At this stage, the Secretary for the Civil Service, representing the government, gave his final defence of the government's handling of the matter:

The Government is in full support of the broad principle that it must remain accountable to the Legislative Council. However, I must at the same time add that we must be given sufficient management authority. This should cover our authority under relevant rules and regulations to employ, transfer and dismiss individual civil servants. Lastly, we must be given the authority to maintain the effective operation of the Government's management and investigation systems and this will involve applications for Court rulings for the protection of public interests (*Legislative Council Minutes*, 18th June 1997).

Issues and Lessons

A number of issues can be identified in the case described in this chapter. First, it is obviously a matter of personnel management, in which the policy secretary in charge of the Civil Service Branch tried to make and implement a decision regarding the resignation of a senior public servant. It was conducted with public interest in mind, and the decision to waive the twelve-month notice period could be seen as appropriate in view of the high level of uncertainty and major changes taking place in society as well as in the Civil Service. If the decision had been implemented without an outcry from the media and the public, it could be considered as a routine administrative situation.

Public managers in Hong Kong have been making such major decisions without facing the need to explain or elaborate for a long time. Thus, the "liberation management approach" (Terry, 1998, 195) appears to have worked well, as highly-skilled and committed public managers knew how to manage. However, the crisis was precipitated as Hong Kong had been moving beyond that stage and had entered an era of democratic governance under which decisions and actions had to be presented, explained and defended publicly. A traditional bureaucracy, unfamiliar with the requirements of the new demands, only succeeded in escalating the problem, which reached crisis proportions with the constant refusal of the government to come to terms with the changed circumstances. The Hong Kong Government insisted on applying its traditional management style; making arbitrary decisions and informing only the outcome to the public without providing reason or rationale.

The government could not anticipate the emergence of a crisis due to its lack of understanding of the new environment. Therefore, the warning signs, such as initial reports on the unusual nature of the retirement, were ignored and the public service was hit with sudden impact. It did not emerge as a "serious threat to basic social, institutional and organizational interests and structures" as described by Rosenthal and Kouzmin (1991), but could definitely be interpreted as a sign of the changing times.

The case exposed Hong Kong, perhaps for the first time, to the danger of a direct confrontation between the executive and the legislature. Hong Kong bureaucracy, long used to dominating the administrative process, had a difficult time accepting and responding to criticism from the representatives of the public. Bureaucratic intransigence was prominent throughout the duration of the case, and it reflected the refusal of the public officials to recognise the legitimacy of the Legislative Council and share power with it. Repeated denial of any impropriety in the case by the senior civil servants, with full support from the Governor, reflected a complete lack of responsiveness in managing public services. It became increasingly obvious that the government's emphasis on more transparency and consultation were mere rhetoric, and raised serious doubts about the definition and articulation of public interest in Hong Kong. This had an impact on the level of public confidence in the system.

In many ways, the public confidence crisis was generated by the public service through its handling of the retirement case. A refusal to come to terms with reality, combined with reluctance to disclose information to the highest political institution, resulted in a crisis of confidence in the government. The process of management appeared to be concentrated on a steadfast refusal to admit irregularities and mistakes, and repeated assertions that public interest could be best defined and upheld by the bureaucracy, without any participation by other institutions such as the legislature and the media.

In view of the lack of consensus regarding the substance of public interest, Harmon tried to redefine the concept. Since various groups in society participate in determining what constitutes public interest, the emphasis was shifted from substance, to the process of upholding it. Thus, "...public interest is the continually changing outcome of political activity among individuals and groups within a democratic political system" (Harmon, 1992: 51). But such an approach was not to be found in Hong Kong, where the balance of power was tilted heavily towards the bureaucracy.

The end result has been the exposure of a number of weaknesses in the public services. Although the existing political and administrative arrangements allowed the government to hold its ground, the long-term impacts will be difficult to ignore. There is no doubt that in the future, decisions of such nature will have to be made in a much more transparent manner, and open communication with the public and their representatives will be essential to manage such crises of confidence. Public officials will have to realise that promotion of public confidence in the system is a useful method of containing crises and managing them.

3 Managing Public Information

The issue of information in public management has been a sensitive area for many reasons. Traditionally, governments did not feel obliged to inform the public of their plans and actions, and most decisions were made in an arbitrary manner. With the development of liberal democratic systems, the exchange of information and increased communication between government and citizens has become the order of the day. However, many governments are not completely comfortable with this arrangement, and public managers in particular find it an additional burden on their workload. It is also believed that the public is either not interested or not capable of comprehending and utilising all information released by the government. Moreover, officials may even consider it necessary not to release for the consumption of the public all information on policies and administration. Hence, public managers may not appreciate the need for keeping the public informed about governmental operations.

"The push for participation by all kinds of people, and the inherent leakiness of the information resource, combine to produce the modern executive's most puzzling dilemma" (Cleveland, 1992: 371). As an information society matures, it is possible to obtain information from a variety of sources. Unless the government adopts a free and open approach to the dissemination of information, alternative sources could lead the propagation of messages, from which it may not be possible to restore the confidence of the public. When a crisis is encountered, the public looks towards the government for guidance and action. The tradition of executive-led administration in Hong Kong has resulted in an expectation of strong leadership by the government in resolving crises. Unfortunately, this element was not visible during the case under study and the inability to collate and manage information emerged as a major weakness of public sector managers.

Management of public health is one of the most important tasks of modern governments. The foremost requirement is to provide medical care for the large number of citizens who may suffer from a variety of illnesses. Since this service consumes a considerable amount of public resources, to increase efficiency and effectiveness, most governments have to concentrate on preventive measures. One of the major trends of building a developed health care system is the empowerment of the patient to improve their own lifestyle and health. Increased accessibility to information and the emphasis on public education has widened the government's role as a responsible disseminator of vital health news. In some cases however, the government structure may not facilitate the new role.

In keeping with recent developments in public services management, public managers are performing an increasingly wide range of functions. As research and development expand our understanding of the world around us, enriching us with magnified detail, so also must the number of management positions expand and develop. The basic functions of our conventional public service managers remain, but the intricate nature of modern public management has complicated the roles and responsibilities of the officials. Dynamics of government structure need to accommodate heightened awareness of the latest developments, and alertness of possible overlaps of new roles created to match new ideas and functions. Therefore, the management of public health has emerged as a major challenge to the capabilities of public managers, who may not always be prepared to deal with the numerous problems that confront them. A critical area is the provision of information and establishing an effective system of communication with the public.

Crises may erupt in many ways. The formulation of public policies is influenced by numerous considerations, and errors of judgement in anticipating problems and ensuring adequate measures can lead to criticism. In running health programs, financial capability plays a major role, but the values of quality, accessibility and distribution must be upheld at the same time. In many countries, the major stakeholders -- medical practitioners, caregivers and support service providers, and the pharmaceutical industry -- participate in various activities to promote their own interests. Public managers are required to strike a balance between the demands and needs of these groups and the consumers of such services, as well as perform the task of regulation so that an acceptable health service can be provided.

The Case

The following case illustrates the complexity involved in managing health crises in the public sector and the confusion and uncertainty that affected its management. The problem started with the death of a three-year old boy in May 1997. He was afflicted with an apparently common illness which had all the symptoms of the viral flu and died at Queen Elizabeth Hospital in

Hong Kong. Following standard procedures in such cases, the hospital forwarded a specimen to the Department of Health laboratories for examination.

Several tests were conducted on the specimen obtained from the boy, and the virus was identified as an Influenza A variety. Reagents normally applied by the World Health Organization, however, could not identify the strain of the virus. The chief virologist of the Department of Health, Dr. Wilna Lim, forwarded the sample to three international laboratories -- the Center for Disease Control in the United States of America, Mill Hill in the United Kingdom, and the National Institute of Health and the Environment in the Netherlands -- for conducting further investigation to identify the strain.

The child's death remained unexplained and efforts continued for several months to unravel the mystery. Tests at the Center for Disease Control were unsuccessful in matching "the virus with any flu strains known to affect humans" (Kennedy School of Government, 1998: 1). After futile attempts to match it with such strains, the other option was to see if it could be matched with strains that cause influenza in animals. The results established that the cause of death was H5N1, a dangerous virus that originated from birds.

The implications of this finding were grave. The H5N1 virus, discovered in South Africa in 1961, was known only to infect various species of birds including chickens and ducks. Conventional virological theory maintains that pigs, because they can be infected with both human and avian viruses, are "mixing vessels" for virus genetic information, generating new strains of disease that can be passed over the species-lines to humans. The H5N1 virus found in the three-year old boy, however, was a "pure avian flu" known only in birds, bringing to question all prior understanding of the transmission of viruses. Scientists were forced to consider for the first time, the possibility of direct bird and human infection from this deadly virus. Managing such a situation required a wide range of skills on the part of public sector managers in Hong Kong.

Informing the Community

The preliminary results of the tests were available on 13th August 1997. The Director of Health, Dr. Margaret Chan, immediately launched a field investigation to uncover details of the case. She said, "we got in touch with the doctors who looked after the case, with the family members, we even got in touch with the [Agriculture and Fisheries Department] AFD" (Mathewson, *South China Morning Post*, 22nd August 1997). It was at this stage that health authorities came to know about the cases of death among Yuen Long chickens. Earlier in February and March, an epidemic had swept across a number of chicken farms in Guangdong Province in China, killing 1.7 million birds and costing farmers more than one million Renmenbi (currency of the People's republic of China; one Renmenbi is equivalent to approximately 12 US cents). In April, the same epidemic killed 4,500 birds in Hong Kong's New Territories (Mathewson, *South China Morning Post*, 22nd August 1997). As the crisis unfolded, the government had to find ways of satisfying public curiosity.

On 18th August, the Department of Health received a written confirmation from the CDC of H5N1 in the sample. Days later, after grappling with the lack of information about the disease and uncertain about a course of action to take, the department held a press conference: "It's not certain at this stage whether or not the virus isolated has any role at all in [the three year old toddler's] death... We have no information to show if [the virus] has jumped directly from bird to human or if it has gone through an intermediary host. This is under investigation" (Moir & Mathewson, *South China Morning Post*, 21st August 1997). Dr. Chan assured that testing and surveillance in government clinics would be stepped up, and officials would work with the World Health Organization to analyze the virus further and develop a vaccine. But this did not help explain the strategies the government were to adopt in dealing with the crisis.

Concurrent with the Department of Health's announcement, the Agriculture and Fisheries Department introduced a number of measures to check poultry imported from China, as well as that supplied by local chicken farms. Dr. Kitman Dyrting, Veterinary Officer of the Agriculture and Fisheries Department stated:

> [S]ince last week when we learnt of the child's death from the virus, our import control section now requires health certificates declaring that the consignment of livestock is healthy and free of the virus. In addition, blood samples are taken from both imported and local chickens for antibody testing" (*Hong Kong Standard,* 22nd August 1997).

International experts from the Center for Disease Control and the World Health Organization and local specialists from the Department of Health, Agriculture and Fisheries Department, the Government Virus Unit, and a number of universities in Hong Kong were quickly assembled to form a taskforce. The objective was to devise a plan of action, and to investigate the source and characteristics of H5N1. "If the virus has gone through major changes—it is called antigenic shift—it may increase the potential for a big epidemic", explained the Director of Health, Dr. Chan (*Reuters News Service*, 20th August 1997). Deputy Director of Health, Dr. Paul Saw Tian-aun, who led the taskforce, said Hong Kong could breathe easy if it was found that the H5N1 virus had not mutated significantly (Benitez & Williams, *Hong Kong Standard*, 21st August 1997).

Public Suspicion about the Source of the Disease

The public, in the meantime, was growing weary from yet another public health scare. The climax of 1997 had been predicted to be the return of Hong Kong to China. However, the "bird flu" and the battle against continuous outbreaks of a number of food related diseases was overshadowing Hong Kong's most important moment. Mei Ng Fong Siu-mei, Director of the voluntary organisation Friends of the Earth argued: "It's about time our Department of Health made community health a top priority. Years ago we were told there were not enough health officers to check and monitor and do regular testing of samples. This should be an important role [in preventing disease outbreaks]". She suggested that the 'filthy environment' was a breeding ground for disease and should be cleaned up (Moir, *South China Morning Post*, 22nd August 1997).

      The poultry industry was becoming increasingly defensive. An indignant owner of a chicken farm in Lau Fau Shan in the New Territories of Hong Kong remarked: "I have been with chickens for more than twenty years. Look, I'm still very healthy, ain't I?" (So, *Hong Kong Standard*, 21st August 1997). Local poultry farmers had been experiencing economic hardship, and they claimed that unrestricted chicken imports from China were the cause of their problems. Thus, they were relieved when a local politician pointed out that over three-quarters of chickens consumed in Hong Kong were imported from China. The public, including senior officials, keen on finding a scapegoat to blame for the disease, were easily convinced by such statements and believed that China was the source of the

H5N1 virus. Later, in January 1998, a special working group consisting of thirteen international experts examined chicken farms in Guangdong Province, and concluded that the virus did not originate from China. They suggested that Hong Kong's farms and markets were the possible sources of the virus.

Government Denial

At a Legislative Council Health Panel Meeting on 8th September 1997, the Deputy Director of Health, Dr. Saw updated the members on the progress of the investigation of the virus. According to him, preliminary analysis of the incident indicated that H5N1 did not seem to pose a threat to public health. He expressed satisfaction with the management of the situation and felt that no special measures were needed. It was announced that the investigation had found no other clinical case of H5N1 and the taskforce had concluded that the first confirmed case of human H5N1 was also an isolated case.

Dr. Daniel Lavanchy, head of the World Health Organization's influenza program and a member of the taskforce formed by the Department of Health, confirmed the findings of the WHO headquarters in Geneva: "It has now been established that the boy died after coming into contact with chickens infected with the H5N1 virus. It seems the boy was in contact with chicken farms where there had been an outbreak of this virus. We now think the idea that the boy got infected from chickens with the H5N1 virus is the most likely link as there is no other hypothesis". He emphasised that researchers were treating the death of the three-year old toddler as an isolated case (Williams, *Hong Kong Standard,* 12th November 1997). On 10th November 1997, the government publicly confirmed the notion that direct contact with an infected chicken was the reason for the infection suffered by the victim.

New Cases

The crisis was nowhere near an end, as was evident from subsequent developments. Within a few days, more cases of the bird flu infection in humans were found, and concern heightened as the seriousness of the crisis was gradually being realised. In November, a two-year-old child was diagnosed with the virus, but the patient recovered. The Deputy Director of Health did not want to admit any relationship between the two cases of May and November. He found no cause for panic and stated "There is no evidence the infection has spread" (Lee, *South China Morning Post,* 29th November 1997).

Such assurance did not help to manage the crisis or alleviate the concern of the public. Over the next few weeks, the list of those infected with the H5N1 virus continued to grow. "All told, by that point, there were nine confirmed bird flu cases, 10 additional suspected cases, three victims in critical condition -- and four dead" (Kennedy School of Government, 1998: 6). The victims were not only young children, and included a 54-year-old man. In the final count, a total of eighteen cases were confirmed, out of which six resulted in deaths (*South China Morning Post,* 31st August 1998). Obviously, the crisis was assuming a much larger proportion than was anticipated at the early stages. A range of necessary tasks aimed at the investigation for determining the cause, managing the crisis and placating the public made the situation increasingly difficult.

Public Anxiety

The population was disconcerted by the news of additional victims of the flu. The second case of infection refuted the notion of the first being a secluded incident, and indicated the active, but invisible, presence of H5N1 in Hong Kong. As a result, a chain of events took place. A large number of patients with any flu-like symptoms flooded the emergency wards of local hospitals, creating strong pressure on the provision of health services. The poultry industry suffered a major setback as prices for chickens dropped and demand decreased. Petting zoos were closed and schools, day care centres and parks prohibited the presence of animals in classrooms and on public display. In some cases, pets were abandoned through the fear that they might transmit the 'bird flu' to their owners.

Doctors and other medical professionals were frustrated at being unable to provide adequate care and information to their patients. "Can it be killed by heat or not?" demanded Jennifer Wan Man-fan, Director of Nutrition at Hong Kong University's disease laboratory. "Tell us the characteristics. Tell us how it multiplies -- they can do this in a laboratory. Where is this data? Will they tell us how the virus cells behave?" (Moir, *South China Morning Post,* 13th December 1997). Legislators were dissatisfied with the Government's management of the situation. "Do our health officials understand that lack of information creates suspicion which often leads to irrational conclusions and even panic?" questioned Liberal

Party legislator, Ronald Arculli (*South China Morning Post,* 18th December 1997).

All of these questions were legitimate. The government's assurance of the virus infection being an isolated case could not be accepted any more. The dissemination of incorrect information, combined with a lack of effort to set the record straight led to additional anxieties among the public. The managers of public health in Hong Kong had failed to provide adequate and pertinent information on the origin, transmission, treatment, and containment of the virus. There was hardly any advice and guidance for the victims, let alone for the general public. The worst aspect of the crisis was the confused and helpless stance adopted by the government. Here was no coherent explanation of the situation confronting Hong Kong, and no information on the government's strategy for dealing with it.

Government Response

The government was clearly perplexed with the task of addressing public anxiety over the crisis. Dr. Keiji Fukuda, of the Center for Disease Control and a member of the international taskforce, admitted that researchers were baffled by the constantly-changing method of transmission of the virus: "In this instance, we know something is going on, but we don't know much about it" (Hutchings, *Daily Telegraph,* 17th December 1997). In the same way, the mysteries surrounding the disease also puzzled the government. The prevailing circumstances and the lack of a clear plan for managing the crisis prevented the government from complying with requests for providing more information. Since the start of the crisis, the Department of Health had dutifully held regular press conferences, updating their WebPages with any new data concerning the bird flu. The Deputy Director of Health tried to defend the actions taken by his department: "Apart from information supplied to the media, information and advice to doctors on H5N1 was also made available through the Internet and direct mail" (*South China Morning Post,* 20th December 1997). Progress of all on-going investigations, however, had been slow. But the most formidable problem was that the government simply did not have the information required and requested by the public. The weakness of the strategy was evident from the fact that the process of communication with the public remained ineffective.

The government's only viable alternative was to continually broaden surveillance in the hope that it would prevent, or at least stall, further transmission of the virus until more conclusive data could be obtained. Even this task appeared to be a tall order. Efforts at achieving this end were complicated by the involvement of an increasing number of government departments who had found the bird flu relevant to their portfolio. Co-ordination of activities of all these agencies became a formidable task. Overlapping responsibilities and ineffective communication among agencies resulted in conflicting information and clumsy piecemeal efforts against the virus, although these were described as "stepped up measures". The government was in a no-win situation. It appeared that they were neither able to contain the mysterious disease, nor curb the increasingly intensifying public hysteria and concern over its origin and impact. Nevertheless, Dr. Leong Chee-hung, the legislator representing the medical constituency, continued to press the government for more information and clues regarding policy decisions that were to be made in response to the crisis. The government had no answers to the numerous questions raised by the public, medical professionals, the poultry industry and other stakeholders.

On 11th December 1997, a comment by the Director of Health, Dr. Margaret Chan, changed the way the public viewed government competence in the management of the H5N1 threat. In her own endeavour to soothe concerns, Dr. Chan offhandedly said that chicken was safe to eat and added that she still ate it on a daily basis (Lee Wei Man, *Apple Daily,* 12th December 1997). This was an unfortunate statement to make considering the level of anxiety over the issue prevailing at the time. The Director of Health was intensely criticised for such a comment. "[Dr. Chan's statement showed] irresponsible behavior in someone who should have calmed public concerns by disclosing what measures her department would adopt immediately to prevent the spread of the virus and how ordinary citizens could protect themselves", wrote Lo Shiu-hing in a letter to the *South China Morning Post* on 30th December 1997. *AsiaWeek* (30th January 1998) considered Chan's statement to be "out-of-touch and useless in quelling Hong Kong fears".

Margaret Chan's deputy made an effort at containing damage after the publication of her statement. Dr. Saw observed that "Her intention was to reassure, in laymen's terms. After all, it is correct to say that eating cooked chicken does not pose a risk. But her statement that "I eat chicken every day" was inappropriate, overkill in the sense that no person would be eating chicken 365 days a year, and it's illogical to expect the community to believe in a statement of that nature. It is important to reassure within the context of the prevailing evidence, in a context that's believable. Especially when you are talking as a professional" (Kennedy School of Government,

1998: 5). The statements by the Director and Deputy Director of Health reflected the lack of a co-ordinated and coherent approach for resolving the crisis. It can be assumed that the gap in thinking and communication would be much higher among the various agencies involved in the process. More damage was inflicted to the image of the Civil Service, which had already come under scrutiny several times since 1997.

In the face of continuous questioning, the Office of the Chief Executive inadvertently conceded that chicken had been removed from Tung Chee-hwa's (the Chief Executive of Hong Kong SAR) meals in fear that he would contact H5N1 (Ho, *South China Morning Post,* 6th January 1998). This confused the public further. While the Director of Health stated that she dined on chicken "365 days a year", the Chief Executive was shunning it for fear of infection. The blatant contrast of views and strategies between two major public figures regarding the transmissibility of the bird flu spurred widespread criticism of the government and the understanding and abilities of the leadership.

At a meeting of the Legislative Council Health Services Panel held on 9th December 1997, Democratic Alliance for the Betterment of Hong Kong (a pro-China political party) member and provisional legislator, Chan Yuen-han, pleaded with the government to set up a working group which could help to more efficiently handle new information concerning the bird flu. She thought that the group would be able to educate the public on preventive measures and ensure that only the most accurate and up to date information would be publicised (*Minutes of Health Services Panel Meeting* on 9th December 1997). "Given the psychological state of the public [the Government] should be more forthcoming with information. People are worried", she said (Sui, *Hong Kong Standard,* 10th December 1997).

The government formed a working group and appointed the Chief Secretary, Mrs. Anson Chan, to be the leader of a new interdepartmental taskforce responsible for keeping the public informed about the management of the crisis. The Chief Secretary had kept a low profile during the course of the crisis, and apparently allowed the government officials from the relevant departments a free hand at dealing with it. However, criticism of the government's mismanagement of the crisis was intensifying. The government sought to salvage the situation by getting important public figures involved in the process. It appeared that it was hoping to redeem its poor public relations management by cashing in on the image and popularity of the Chief Secretary. Although the exact duties of the new taskforce were uncertain and not spelled out, the mere idea of having Mrs. Chan in charge put the public at ease. It did not matter that

Mrs. Chan's involvement in the management of the bird flu crisis remained minimal even after the announcement.

Reaction of the Poultry Industry

The poultry industry, in the meantime, was no longer content with passively watching the market for chicken decline. After a number of discussions with government representatives, wholesalers acquired the support of the Agriculture and Fisheries Department to close down Cheung Sha Wan Temporary Wholesale Poultry Market to allow for a massive cleanup and sterilisation operation over a period of five days. Such a move was expected to calm public fears and to win back confidence in the industry. Meanwhile, imports totalling at least 80,000 chickens daily were reduced by one-third to cope with the facility being closed (Ng, *South China Morning Post,* 15th December 1997).

The circumstances reflected the failure of measures taken by the government to effectively identify the causes of the crisis and respond to them. In spite of apparent attempts and occasional statements to indicate the continued efforts to manage the crisis, no concrete action was evident. As a consequence, various sections of the public became frustrated. In particular, one of the major stakeholders, the poultry merchants, had to consider ways and means to survive in the face of this grave challenge to their livelihood.

Chicken farmers, in their own effort to keep their businesses afloat, negotiated with the Agriculture and Fisheries Department to slaughter every chicken in Hong Kong to eliminate all traces of the virus. Farmers claimed that they were no longer able to support their flocks due to declining demand caused by the bird flu scare. Mak Yip-shing, spokesman for the Hong Kong Farmers' Association said, "The drastic move [the slaughter] will certainly push farmers to hardship and we hope the Government could offer them compensation so that they can start chicken farming all over again" (*South China Morning Post,* 21st December 1997). The AFD refuted the suggestion saying it was unnecessary and unhelpful since the majority of chickens consumed in Hong Kong were imported from China. Later, farmers again met with AFD representatives in the hope of obtaining an official statement that the bird flu could not be contracted through eating chicken. The government refused to issue such a statement, and made it clear that such an assertion would only be made if tests on the birds proved to be negative.

Another stakeholder in the case, the People's Republic of China, was also contemplating action. On Christmas Eve 1998, Beijing's Ministry of Foreign Trade and Economic Relations ordered a temporary prohibition on poultry exports to Hong Kong. Earlier in the week, Guangdong Department of Agriculture announced that they would quarantine all export poultry while conducting random checks on farms to ensure hygiene standards. They followed up their action by guaranteeing that all chickens bound for Hong Kong would carry certificates of health issued by mainland investigators before export. It was finally decided, however, that a ban would give Hong Kong the time to formulate a system for ensuring virus-free birds, during which the AFD planned to conduct massive inspections of Hong Kong's 160 chicken farms and to test all birds within the territory for the virus. Two markets, one in Ap Lei Chau and one in Cheung Sha Wan, had been confirmed to be infected with H5N1 and the ban allowed for widespread disinfecting of many of Hong Kong's markets. Guangnan Group, a major poultry supplier supported the move and its spokesman Lee Sau-ping said, "it is no good keeping importing chickens when no one wants to buy them" (Ng, *South China Morning Post*, 24th December 1997).

While all kinds of measures were being taken to minimise the risk to public health through their consumption of chicken, the industry was incurring a huge loss. The interests of one of the major stakeholders, the poultry industry, appeared to be neglected as the government contemplated various measures for ensuring the supply of infection-free poultry for local consumers. Meanwhile, the inability of the government to provide the public with detailed and systematic information on the crisis continued to add to the confusion.

International Reaction to the Crisis

In the international arena, the bird flu case was attracting a great deal of attention. Since the widely publicised outbreak of the Ebola virus in Africa years earlier, the world had become more sensitive to new and unusual diseases and the communication of germs. Many believed that such viruses had become highly mobile and could enter new locations due to the rapid change of transportation technology. The deterioration of the world environment was identified as another factor that contributed to the problem. This had substantial implications for Hong Kong. There was the possibility of viruses being transmitted through travellers who might carry them without being aware of it. As a huge number of people undertake international travel, this was considered to be an area of risk.

Many governments started advising travellers from their countries to take extra precaution on trips to Hong Kong. The territory earns a substantial percentage of its revenue from the tourism industry, and the travel advisory had a devastating effect. Newspapers reported posters being raised in Taiwanese airports warning potential tourists away from Hong Kong. It was also reported that President Fidel Ramos of the Philippines issued a handwritten directive to the Departments of Foreign Affairs and Health ordering them to 'monitor carefully' Hong Kong's bird flu outbreak "to ensure that there is no spread of this 'bird flu' to the Philippines". Tourist arrivals plunged 26 per cent in December 1997 against arrivals a year earlier, to 840,000 (Robles, *South China Morning Post,* 30th December 1997).

Resolution of the Crisis

The time had arrived for the government to take decisive action. Finding no other way of alleviating public anxiety and ensuring the elimination of virus-infected chickens, drastic action was considered. The culling or slaughter of all chickens in Hong Kong was thought to be the strategy for dealing with the problem. In one sweep, every chicken in Hong Kong would be killed and this would ensure that no infected stock remained in the territory. "[T]he Hong Kong government issued a death sentence on every chicken in the city. The radical measure was a desperate attempt to contain H5N1, the flu virus that had suddenly leapt from fowl to people" (*AsiaWeek*, 30th January 1998). This is an extremely unusual decision and there must have been hesitation and reservations among the group, which finally chose this option.

The act of killing all the chickens would invariably be messy and complex and the action would be taken more in hope than in a rational spirit. Co-ordination of the operation had to be made, and several arrangements needed to be in place for disposing of the carcasses after the culling. Moreover, it entailed huge additional costs. Providing compensation to chicken farmers and others in the poultry industry would be enormously expensive. However, there seemed to be no other way for demonstrating the decisiveness and sincerity of the government, which expected that this would put the public's mind at ease.

At daybreak on 28th December, the Agriculture and Fisheries Department declared two more venues -- another section of the Cheung Sha

Wan Temporary Poultry Market and a chicken farm in Yuen Long -- as infected areas under the *Public Health (Animal and Birds) Regulation*. The evidence of spreading infection was too salient for the government to ignore and speedy action was required. Hours later a plan, sanctioned by the Chief Executive, was announced to slaughter all 1.2 million chickens in Hong Kong in a 24-hour operation starting at 1 p.m. on 29th December 1997.

It was decided that the total "compensation to all those involved in the process of raising and selling chickens would amount to $30 per bird. Agriculture authorities believed the total cost would be manageable. In addition, they hoped the slaughter might be completed in relatively short order" (Kennedy School of Government, 1998:7). The plan was laid out in detail: chickens would be captured, placed in plastic containers and gassed with carbon dioxide; carcasses would then be disinfected, bagged and disposed of in landfills. The Secretary for Economic Services, Stephen Ip Shu-kwan, confidently stated "No matter how remote they [the birds] are, they will all be covered in this exercise" (*South China Morning Post,* 29th December 1997).

The action could not be executed as planned and the information given by the government turned out to be inaccurate yet again. The twenty-four hour target proved too ambitious. It was only on the morning of 29th December that the logistics of the plan were discussed and supplies gathered. Complications had not been considered in the original plan, and the operation was set back by insufficient gear and experience. Hundreds of government workers dispatched for the job needed to learn within a few hours the slaughter techniques determined by the government. Public health and agriculture authorities, working together, had to create a temporary army of poultry executioners. None of these public officials could be considered technically or attitudinally suitable for the job. "A bunch of pen-pushers and techies were plucked from comfortable desks and ordered to kill more than a million living creatures" (*AsiaWeek,* 30th January 1998). The Director of the Agriculture and Fisheries Department ruefully commented: "This is a special and unprecedented task. I believe 98 of every 100 staff have never even touched a live chicken before. They have to catch the chickens one by one from cages and learn how to administer the gas" (Lee, *South China Morning Post,* 31st December 1997). By 9:00 p.m. on December 29th, only 20% of the entire estimated poultry population had been slaughtered. In the end, controversies erupted over the strategy adopted to deal with the crisis. "...[C]ritics assailed it for being too little, too late, a media ploy and, finally, a botched job when supposedly dead poultry were spotted running around loose..." (*AsiaWeek,* 30th January 1998).

Low Profile of the Chief Executive

On New Year's Eve, the Chief Executive, Tung Chee-hwa, made a visit to the already-emptied Cheung Sha Wan Poultry Market. Since the outbreak of the bird flu, he had remained aloof, neither appearing at any infection-site nor speaking publicly about the disease. At this particular visit, the media anticipated that Tung was finally ready to face the public to talk about the issue and they were eager to interrogate him about his evasiveness. Tung's spokeswoman fervently defended his silence and said: "He has been kept informed on the matter" (*South China Morning Post,* 1st January 1998). Tung avoided speaking about his responsibilities as Chief Executive, and simply made a vague statement without going into the depth of the crisis affecting Hong Kong: "[The Bird Flu] is an issue that all of us in the Government are very concerned about. It is an issue that has been dealt with a great deal of intensity by my colleagues standing on my right and left [the Director of Health and the Secretary for Economic Services]... It is understandable that the public criticizes the way we have handled the issue... but there are areas where the improvements need to be made and we are going to make those improvements. We are looking at these things very urgently. We hope these will all be sorted out" (*South China Morning Post,* 1st January 1998).

Inevitably this appearance and the useless statement by Tung drew intense criticism over the next few days. Sensing his lack of confidence and comfort in the face of a crisis, newspaper editorials questioned the leadership abilities of the new Chief Executive. The *Apple Daily* wrote: "What are you doing with your time Mr. Tung? No one is asking Mr. Tung to eat chicken in public to show there is no need to panic about the bird flu... but ...[he] should at least let people know that he is concerned about the issue and about public health" (*South China Morning Post,* 1st January 1998). Other newspapers ruthlessly compared the new Chief Executive with the ex-Governor, "Former Gov. Chris Patten would have immediately visited any major accident scene" (Sly, *Chicago Tribune,* 7th January 1998). "He [Governor Chris Patten] would have waded into the markets and throttled them with his own hands" (*Economist Intelligence Unit,* 12th January 1998).

Such comparison with his predecessor was a telling commentary on the performance of the Chief Executive and his public officials. As Hong Kong was basking in the glory of uninterrupted economic success for several decades, an apparently minor problem shortly after the withdrawal of the British from the territory had exposed the weakness of the administrative machinery and its leadership. The lack of communication between the government and the public revealed that the style and nature of administration had not really changed in spite of several proclamations on reforming the bureaucracy and changing its culture.

Errors in the Operation

Five days after the target deadline, while the slaughter continued, errors in the operation became increasingly apparent. Some interesting facts emerged at this stage. It was found that the system of record keeping was inadequate, and 68 registered farms were found which were unlisted in original government documents. Seventy thousand extra chickens unaccounted for were killed in the operation. Another 20,000 were found in illegal chicken 'hotels' and wholesale farms. Staff dispatched to gather dead carcasses struggled to keep up with the mass culling, leaving tons of dead chickens in the streets, and many were exposed to open air due to tears in plastic bags or procedural errors. Streams of blood flowed onto the streets. Stray animals and rats were found scavenging around the bags on the roadside. Newspaper reports threw the effectiveness of the slaughter into doubt as scientists confirmed that though chickens infected with H5N1 were culled, the real harbingers of the disease were ducks, geese and other species of waterfowl. Anxiety kept on rising and the public continued to look for an explanation for the errors committed in dealing with this problem.

The Chief Executive's response to the situation was typical. He acknowledged the validity of criticism from the public over the management of the problem. His vague comment on the need for an expression of commitment to make improvements hardly helped in restoring the image of the public officials. The statement was similar to that made earlier, and practically said or did nothing to instil confidence in the minds of the public.

The Director of the AFD, on the other hand, apologised for the problems, "I was directing the operation in the field...If my presence could not avoid any mistakes, I should take the blame because I was there...If my resignation is going to solve the problem, I will consider it" (*South China Morning Post,* 1ˢᵗ January 1998). Chief Secretary, Mrs. Anson Chan refuted the suggestion, insisting that there was no need for the resignation of any senior civil servants: "the operation was an extremely difficult task...and colleagues from various departments tried very hard working day and night...I hope the public and members of the Provisional

Legislative Council will be aware of their efforts" (Wan & No, *South China Morning Post,* 4th January 1998).

Assessment of the Strategy

The government was in drastic need of demonstrating its ability to respond to the crisis. The controversy gradually subsided and some anxieties were alleviated through the introduction of tough new measures for hygiene control intended to protect public health. At the same time, a comprehensive system was devised for the importation of poultry into Hong Kong. The issue of providing compensation had to be negotiated with poultry industry representatives, and this required considerable skill and judgement. The industry agreed that with the introduction of higher standards, new equipment and techniques were necessary to ensure appropriate results. After intense bargaining, the government finally gave in to the pressure for increased compensation and for more flexible loans. The entire package was to cost a whopping HK$770 million from the public exchequer. The Legislative Council approved the compensation and loan package on 9th January 1998.

No new cases of H5N1 were detected over the next few days. Consequently, on 11th January 1998, the Director of Health declared that the slaughter of the chickens had been a success (Lee, *South China Morning Post,* 12th January 1998). A week and a half later, 6th February was designated as the date when imports of chickens from China would resume. It was also announced that imports of ducks and geese would come at a later date. The statement by the Director of Health, the lack of new cases of infection, and the announcement of the resumption of imports of chicken put the minds of the public at ease. They were relieved at the news and, as a sign of confidence in the newly-rebuilt poultry industry, the first batch of imported chicken after the bird flu crisis was immediately sold out (Ng & Chan, *South China Morning Post,* 9th February 1998).

There was widespread dissatisfaction and confusion over the management of the bird flu crisis. However, a year after the slaughter, the Director of Health, and a Hong Kong University professor, Dr. Kennedy Shortridge, were awarded Thailand's Mahildol Award for their contribution towards public health. It would be interesting to see the kind of accolades the successful management of the bird flu crisis would have brought the public sector managers of Hong Kong.

The H5N1 virus did not appear again in Hong Kong after the mass slaughter, but its impact had major consequences for the Special Administrative Region government. Several months after the operation, a consultation was conducted to seek public consensus on the proposed plan to dismantle the Urban and Regional councils in favour of a centralised food hygiene department. The government had received a significant blow in confidence as it struggled to co-ordinate the many bureaus and departments connected with the area of food and environmental sanitation. The Urban and Regional councils were both attributed with the responsibility of localised hygiene in wet markets and in a number of other public areas. Although it evoked controversy, the plan was generally accepted and in January 2000, Hong Kong saw the creation of the new Environment and Food Hygiene Department. This could be seen as a positive consequence of the crisis.

Issues and Lessons

This chapter has described a case in which a virus that was known to be transmitted among birds and poultry led to death in humans. Since little medical evidence was available about its causes and means of transmission to human beings, the medical authorities of Hong Kong were unable to conduct an appropriate and comprehensive investigation that could resolve the problem and alleviate public anxiety. In view of the uncertainty associated with the case, the government could have chosen a maximum health management strategy that typically minimises public risk. This could have been accomplished by making a quick decision to implement the mass slaughtering of chickens.

As the government pondered over the costs and benefits of such an action, various other considerations entered the equation. Extermination of the entire chicken population in the interest of public health would make the government liable for paying compensation to the poultry industry. Thus, they appeared reluctant to exercise this option as the best choice due to reservations over the issue of providing compensation to the poultry industry. Hence, the first issue raised by the bird flu crisis is the type of risk that should be borne by governments when public health is concerned. In such situations of serving the interests of the public and the industry, it can be argued that "precautionary risk", described by Shrader-Frechette as Type-II (Public) Risks, should receive priority over Type I (Industry) Risks (1991).

A second issue that arises from the case is the importance of public relations in the dissemination of information. The SAR Government, and its Chief Executive in particular, exposed their incompetence in allaying public fears. Their behaviour and actions hardly inspired the confidence of the public in the capability of public managers in Hong Kong. Instead of devising a comprehensive strategy to deal with the crisis and communicating it to all the stakeholders, the acts of the government appeared to be piecemeal and without direction. In the end, the crisis was seen as one that resolved itself without much contribution from public officials.

The role of the two major agencies involved in the process of managing the crisis appeared to be in isolation. While the Department of Health was highly visible at the early stages of the crisis, its actions were found to be concentrated on the search for medical answers to the origin and transmission of the virus. This approach neglected another critical dimension of work expected from the department. There was little effort aimed at informing and reassuring the public and winning their confidence for the government. The provision of inadequate and incorrect information had a negative impact on the image of the government, and public concern could not be addressed.

On the other hand, the Agriculture and Fisheries Department were in the spotlight towards the later stage of the crisis. This agency had to bear the brunt of executing the dubious decision of culling a huge number of chickens without the benefit of relevant skill and training. Although their efforts at catching and killing chickens provided brief moments of amusement for the anxious public watching the proceedings, it delivered a negative image of the hitherto "super efficient" Hong Kong bureaucracy. The degree of communication and co-operation between the two departments was never clear and it is likely that the operation could have been affected by such complications.

A third issue in relation to public management is the poor planning of the eventual chicken slaughter, and insufficient co-ordination among government departments based on a functional division of work. It was over-ambitious on the part of government officials to aim at a 24-hour completion and to exterminate all chickens in the territory. The time limit proved to be unrealistic, as gear and equipment needed to be distributed and staff had to be provided with basic training for the task at hand. Moreover, two different government departments, the Agriculture and Fisheries Department, and the Urban/Regional Services Department respectively, were given the separate tasks of killing chickens and the disposal of carcasses.

The case exposes a weakness of public management in a number of areas. Admittedly, the sudden emergence of an unknown virus made the case much more difficult to deal with. However, the manner in which the public managers considered the options and finally responded with drastic action reflects the lack of a sense of understanding of the delicate balance required in delivering public services. Tough and appropriate decisions have to be made and timing is critical, but the need to maintain a calm and controlled appearance is equally important. In the case of a sensitive area such as public health, public managers have to demonstrate sensitivity to the needs and anxieties of the public. Providing constant and updated information in a clear and coherent manner could ensure this.

In managing public services, unpleasant and unpopular choices often have to be made. The preparation of the public psyche for such decisions is an essential skill for public managers. With total disregard to this vital strategy, public officials were found to make vague and frivolous statements. It was obvious that they were out of their depth in this case and were not sure of the strategies to be adopted in containing the crisis and limiting damage. It was also necessary to take appropriate measures to ensure the return of normalcy once the critical period of danger was over. The case provides a good illustration of the importance of using and managing information in an effective manner to limit the extent of damage from a crisis.

4 Managing Public Confidence

Citizens of modern countries are dependent on the state and government for an increasing number of services. Huge amounts of tax revenue are spent in managing the countries and providing a wide range of services. In reciprocation, citizens expect to live under a system that is fair and provides equal treatment to all. The rule of law has been a prominent concept in the evolution of modern polities, and ensures just and equitable treatment to citizens. Additionally, "The rule of law promises predictability in social life by placing constitutional limits on the kinds of powers that governments may legitimately exercise, as well as on the extent of those governmental powers" (Shapiro, 1994, p. 1). Thus, the concept of rule of law serves to protect the rights and interests of citizens as well as providing a guideline for the actions of governments.

One of the major areas of concern in the reversal of sovereignty from Britain to China has been the continuation of the rule of law in Hong Kong. As different legal traditions are followed in the two countries, Hong Kong was considered to be in danger of suffering in the transition from one to the other. In addition, the nature of the political systems added to the anxieties. As the reforms towards democratisation were being rolled back and the elected legislature scrapped, there was widespread concern over the lack of checks and balances to ensure good government. Ways and means had to be determined for ensuring that the rule of law continued in Hong Kong while it operated as a Special Administrative Region of the People's Republic of China. *The Basic Law* (1990) sought to alleviate these concerns by provision of Article 8: "The laws previously in force in Hong Kong, that is, the common law, rules of equity, ordinances, subordinate legislation and customary law shall be maintained, except for any that contravene this Law, and subject to any amendment by the legislature of the Hong Kong Special Administrative Region". Although such an assurance helped to assuage concerns to some extent, it remained to be seen how the system operated after the handover in 1997. The case in which senior employees of a local newspaper, the *Hong Kong Standard*, were prosecuted emerged as a major test of confidence in the effectiveness of the rule of law in Hong Kong.

The Case

This case discusses a public confidence crisis in relation to the application of the rule of law. The rule of law and the independence of the judiciary have been cornerstones of the birth of the SAR and the successful implementation of one country, two systems. The rule of law, underpinned by an independent legal system, is central to Hong Kong's market economy. It is also a precondition of Hong Kong's economic and political relations with foreign states and international institutions. Since the Basic Law establishes Hong Kong as a separate economic and legal jurisdiction, it allows the territory its own arrangements with foreign states for mutual legal assistance, trade and investment. For the same reason, it is able to be a member of international organisations such as the World Trade Organization, World Bank and the International Labour Organization. Threats to its independent and separate jurisdiction jeopardise such arrangements vital to its prosperity (Ghai, *Far Eastern Economic Review,* 13th January 2000).

The rule of law legitimises the acts and procedures of a directly elected government. Any violation against the rule of law encroaches upon the legitimacy of the government and ultimately on their popular support (Ghai, *South China Morning Post,* 22nd March 1998). It serves as the guarantor of legal rights for citizens and a measure of government accountability. It was felt that any suggestion that it was under threat, particularly within the first year after the change of sovereignty, would result in an uproar and renew the tension and anxiety suffered by Hong Kong throughout the previous decade.

On 17th March 1998, the Secretary for Justice for the Government of Hong Kong, Elsie Leung, levelled charges of fraud against three executives of the *Hong Kong Standard* newspaper (the Standard) based on investigations by the Independent Commission Against Corruption (ICAC). The General Manager, Finance Manager, and former Circulation Director of the newspaper were charged to have daily printed an excess number of newspapers to inflate the circulation figures. According to the charge sheet, this was done for the purpose of deceiving purchasers of advertisement space. The fourth person being named as a co-conspirator in the ICAC file was the owner of the holding company, Sally Aw Sian. However, the Secretary for Justice, without explanation, did not press charges against Sally Aw. According to the ICAC, the three *Hong Kong Standard* employees had "conspired together with Ms. Aw to defraud purchasers of advertising space", positively identifying Aw as a participant in the crime (*Asian Wall Street Journal*, 25th March 1998).

The Vice Chairman of the Hong Kong Bar Association observed that the "[non-prosecution was] unusual, normally what the ICAC says to the Department of Justice attracts great respect. Their decisions are very rarely over-ridden" (Fraser, *South China Morning Post,* 19th March 1998). A senior ICAC source informed the *South China Morning Post,* "We think it was the opinion of many in the Department of Justice, even very senior people, that a prosecution should be brought. It was when it got to the very top that the decision was not made" (Fraser, *South China Morning Post,* 21st January 1999).

The public seemed to view this as a case of discrimination, where a co-conspirator was provided preferential treatment by the government, which did not wish to press charges. They were unable to understand the reasons behind such a decision, and rumours of political favouritism spread rapidly, causing widespread concern over the integrity of the judicial system. It was not a favourable time for the government to enter into a debate on the rule of law and explain the rationale for such an action. In the post-handover period, the public was still uncomfortable with the new arrangements and yet to establish full confidence in the system. They appeared to be suspicious and cautious of the Beijing-appointed government, and were prone to scrutinising every public decision in search of signs of any infringement of the rule of law, and the subsequent interference by the mainland in local society that would follow. Although no signs of direct intervention from Beijing were observed, the scrutiny did uncover the disturbing notion that the Hong Kong government's defence of the rule of law was inherently flawed due to its misunderstanding of its major precepts.

This observation was extended to one of Beijing's appointed elite, Elsie Leung, the Secretary for Justice. It was considered, particularly by the legal profession, that Leung, a family lawyer by training, did not have the most appropriate experience for her role as the government's top lawyer and was ill prepared to act as an authority on prosecution. It was also alleged that her appointment was based more on political considerations than on her competence, in view of her pro-Beijing political involvement as a founding member of the local political party, the Democratic Alliance for the Betterment of Hong Kong (DAB) and as a deputy to the National People's Congress. Although her integrity was never challenged, there were misgivings that her abilities were limited and her loyalties to the Central Government would make her susceptible to political influence and pressure.

It was well known to the Hong Kong people that Aw, the heiress to the Sing Tao media empire, had close links with the political elite in both Hong Kong and in China. The Chief Executive himself was a close family friend. Understandably, he denied any direct involvement with the decision and made the following statement: "[t]he decision to prosecute or not rests entirely with the Secretary for Justice. This is a very fine tradition in Hong Kong. It is also very much provided for in the Basic Law. It's not appropriate for the Chief Executive to interfere. In this case, I think she and her colleagues have considered the case carefully" (*South China Morning Post*, 19th March 1998). Nevertheless, the Chief Executive assured the public to stay confident in the judicial system: "The only point I can emphasize is that Hong Kong's success is because we have a good foundation of the rule of law. Nobody, and I emphasize nobody is above the rule of law. This is our biggest determination" (*Hong Kong Standard*, 20th March 1998). Ironically, the actions of the government did not do much to establish a high level of confidence in the rule of law among citizens.

On 19th March 1998, the Department of Justice tried to dispel misgivings over the Aw case and issued a press statement on their policy of prosecution: "...[o]ur guiding principles are whether the evidence is sufficient to justify a prosecution and, if it is, whether it is in the public interest to bring a prosecution. ...[W]e emphasize that no special treatment was given to any suspects. The status of any suspect or political factors did not feature in our decision...under Article 63 of the Basic Law the Department of Justice controls criminal prosecutions free from any interference. ...It by no means follows that those identified in any alleged conspiracy offence are necessarily charged" (Government Information Services, *Daily Information Bulletin*, 19th March 1998). The press release failed to address concerns, fuelling further speculation and heightening public anxiety.

Issue at Stake

In the absence of an explanation from the government, the Chairman of the Democratic Party and a practising barrister, Martin Lee, sought to publicly define the issue at stake in this case by asking, "When you have a situation where the ICAC decided there is sufficient evidence to warrant a charge, that the three accused had conspired with a fourth one...why is the fourth person left out?" (Humphrey, *Reuters News Services*, 19th March 1998). He reminded the community "The rule of law means no individual or organization is above the law" (*Asiaweek*, 30th March 1998). At the same time, Lee issued a warning that "We mustn't allow people in Hong Kong and people outside Hong Kong to feel that there are two systems of justice, one for the ordinary people and one for the super class" (*South China Morning Post*, 19th March 1998).

Margaret Ng, a former member of the legislature and also a barrister by profession, pointed towards the existence of a depraved judicial system. She wrote that, "Hong Kong prides itself on an open system of justice and fair trial. All those standing charge are presumed innocent until proven guilty" (*South China Morning Post*, 20th March 1998). She argued that if Aw was indeed innocent of fraud, it would be found so in the regular process of justice; but the Secretary for Justice chose to protect Aw and removed the case from the courts, bringing to doubt the independence of the judicial system.

Concerns with the ruling were primarily related to the inconsistencies that affected the case from the beginning. The government failed to refute speculation that political favouritism was involved, and that they had helped Aw get off the list of conspirators in this case. No statement was forthcoming from the government to indicate the legal and procedural reasons for the non-prosecution. Lee and Ng, on the other hand, offered an explanation for the evasive strategy adopted by the government, and it seemed to be reasonable and believable to the public. Their statements also tried to identify the issue at stake and the subsequent direction of debate that would follow. They contended that the rule of law was under threat in Hong Kong. The public, on their part, responded vehemently to the implications. The signs of an imminent crisis were clear.

Redefinition of the Case

On 23rd March 1998, the Secretary for Justice was called to give account at a special meeting for the Provisional Legislative Council's Panel on Administration of Justice and Legal Services. The panel meeting gave Leung an opportunity to explain her stance and to redefine the issue at stake. It would also give her a chance to make the government's position clear and refute charges of misunderstanding and undermining the concept of rule of law. Ironically, this came only two months after the Secretary for Justice had spoken at the first Ceremonial Opening of the Legal Year since the handover, boasting of the "visible evidence of the continuity of Hong Kong's legal traditions", and "the Administration's unwavering commitment to the rule of law in all that it does" (*M2 Presswire*, 13th January 1998).

Statement from the Secretary for Justice

Leung stressed, "[T]he Secretary for Justice, as public prosecutor is not the servant or the tool of the Government" and "should not be subject to the direction and control of the Government and must jealously guard that independence". The independence of the prosecutor extends to "the Police and other law enforcement bodies" such as the ICAC, Leung explained. She stated that the Secretary for Justice prosecutes "not on behalf of the Government but on behalf of the public". "So that when it is claimed that a particular prosecution has been brought, or not brought, for 'political motives' implying that the Secretary for Justice has been told whom to prosecute or not to prosecute...that is completely untrue", she claimed.

According to Leung, the prosecution policy required that "there must be enough evidence to prove all the elements of an offense". She remarked, "There must be a reasonable prospect of securing a conviction because it is not in the interests of public justice, nor of the public revenue that weak or borderline cases should be prosecuted". "If the proposed prosecution survives this evidential test, the prosecutor then has to turn to other criteria, generally known as 'the public interest criteria".

With regard to the decision not to prosecute Sally Aw, Leung assured that she had "strictly adhered to the established prosecution policy...and to Article 63 of the Basic Law". Leung refused to reveal details of the reasons for the non-prosecution, citing "the principle of non-disclosure" and "the fact that three defendants will be on trial" in that case. "I cannot even say whether my decision is based on insufficiency of evidence or the public interest", she said. "This is not the first time that this has occurred...I have been able to identify 13 concluded cases coming from our Commercial Crime Unit alone, in which a named co-conspirator was not charged". Leung continued that, in some cases "where it is alleged that A conspired with B, B's identity ought, where practical, to be revealed in the charge, even if B is not himself charged. B may not be charged, for example, because B may be called as a prosecution witness, is dead, is out of jurisdiction, there is insufficient evidence against B or it is against the public interest to charge B". Along with this complicated explanation, Leung added that the non-prosecution of Aw was not a peculiar or abnormal situation.

The Secretary for Justice concluded her statement to the panel by urging the media and the public to "be patient and place reliance on our open and fair judicial system, as during the trial, the evidence will become open to the public". "As previously indicated, I hope that at the conclusion of the trial it will be possible to make a public statement on the case" (*Government Information Services,* Daily Information Bulletin, 23rd March 1998). The Secretary for Justice said that she would be held responsible if her decision not to prosecute was eventually found to be wrong (Yeung & Hon, *South China Morning Post,* 24th March 1998).

Leung's lengthy statement offered no explanation for the non-prosecution of Aw, other than saying that it was not an unusual case. She appeared before members of the Legislative Council and explained her role as Secretary for Justice as the public prosecutor, reiterated that the policy for prosecution had been faithfully followed, and claimed that her ruling was correct and appropriate. In this way, Leung had indeed redefined the case. Before she made the statement, the concern centred on the government's commitment to the rule of law. Following her statement, the major concern appeared to be related to her ability and suitability to serve as the Secretary for Justice.

Reactions to Leung's statement

Legislators attending the special panel questioned Leung's ability and competence as the Secretary for Justice, raising the concern that her decision-making possibly resulted in a flaw in procedure and a rift in the judicial system. Miriam Lau and Ip Kwok-him raised two issues that received much media attention leading up to the panel meeting. There were rumours that a rift had formed between Leung and the Director of Public Prosecutions, Granville Cross, over the case. In response to these rumours, Leung replied that, "[l]egal advice always differs, this does not mean that we have disagreements" (Loh, *South China Morning Post,* 23rd March 1998). However, the differences did not end there. Within a short period, it was felt that the divergence in opinions was widespread. Even the Secretary for Justice and the ICAC appeared to have different views and opinions. Such complex and confusing developments led the public to believe that the judicial system had become fragmented under the leadership of Elsie Leung, and that the legal system could be adversely affected under the circumstances.

Comments and criticism abounded on the legal and management capability of the Secretary for Justice. Ching wrote: "Since she [the Secretary for Justice] is a civil lawyer with no prosecution experience, it is odd that she overruled career prosecutors, including the Director of Public

Prosecutions. Still if she disagreed with their judgement, she could have asked for a second opinion. This she failed to do" (Ching, *Far Eastern Economic Review*, 9th April 1998). James To, former legislator and practising solicitor, similarly expressed disappointment at the decision of the Secretary for Justice: "People who have years of criminal prosecution experience say that there is sufficient evidence and it is over-ruled by someone who has little or no criminal law experience. It is a disgrace" (Fraser, *South China Morning Post*, 19th March 1998).

Miriam Lau, a legislator representing the Liberal Party, also raised the issue of seeking a second opinion. Lau recalled that there were past cases where the Attorney General had sought legal advice from the private sector after their prosecution decisions had been challenged. She asked if the Secretary for Justice, in view of the uproar the case had caused, had considered seeking legal advice (*Minutes of Special PLC Panel on Administration of Justice and legal Services*, Para.8). The Director of Public Prosecutions, Granville Cross, who accompanied Leung to the panel meeting, responded that legal advice was sought when cases were complex, if a particular area of expertise was needed and unavailable in the department, or if an employee of the department was involved. Following such a policy, the Secretary for Justice claimed that this case was quite simple and legal advice was unnecessary. She also stated:

> The Department of Justice bears the responsibility to decide whether to initiate public prosecutions. I would not be acting independently if I sought a second legal opinion because I feared being criticized by the public. It would not be in line with prosecution principles (Hon, *South China Morning Post*, 24th March 1998).

Lau was not convinced and continued her argument:

> I have to make clear that not every case generates such high public concern. There have been past cases in which the Attorney General sought a second opinion on cases that generated great public concern. Why is it OK in the past but not in this case?" (Hon, *South China Morning Post*, 24th March 1998).

Leung refused to entertain Lau's suggestions and said the case:

> ... has already caused unnecessary worries, and that is not to public interest (*The Asian Wall Street Journal*, 24th March 1998).

Ip Kwok-him of the DAB pursued another line of argument and inquired about the normal procedure taken when differences existed in the views of the Director of Public Prosecutions and the Secretary for Justice (*Minutes of Special Legco Panel on Administration of Justice and Legal Services,* Para. 14). The Director of Public Prosecutions replied that the prosecution policy provided guidance for the handling of cases and as a result, not all cases needed to be referred to the Secretary for Justice unless they were of a sensitive, important or complicated nature. In such a circumstance, Cross said that he would express his opinion on the case, but the Secretary would make the final decision for justice. He said that he respected and supported the decision that Leung had reached regarding Sally Aw (*Minutes of Special Legco Panel on Administration of Justice and Legal Services,* Para. 14-15). Leung also denied that there had been any dispute over the decision for this case between her and the Director of Public Prosecutions (*Minutes of Special Legco Panel on Administration of Justice and Legal Services,* Para. 17 and 20).

It was clear that the session was not going to produce a clear explanation of the decision made by the Secretary for Justice. The public officials appeared to be united in their effort to support the decision. Sensing the futility of proceeding with the session, members of the legislature agreed to pursue the case with the Secretary for Justice again after the trial had concluded. The issue at stake was likely to continue well beyond the length of the trial, and the crisis looming behind the case had to be managed.

Post-trial Complications

The trial of the three executives of the *Hong Kong Standard* came to an end on 20th January 1999. Henrietta So was sentenced to six months in prison and David Wong Wai-shing and Tang Cheong-shing four months each (*South China Morning Post,* 21st January 1999). Although the case of inflating circulation numbers to defraud advertisers had reached a conclusion, public concern over the effectiveness of the rule of law continued to grow. Therefore, in accordance with the decision made before the trial, the Secretary for Justice was invited to make a statement that could possibly give reason for the non-prosecution of Aw. On 4th February, she agreed to appear before the legislators to explain her position.

The Secretary for Justice's Opening Statement

The Secretary for Justice made a long statement to the panel of the Legislative Council with the intention of explaining her decision not to prosecute Aw. She said:

> I am grateful for being given this opportunity to explain my decision not to prosecute Madam [Sally] Aw Sian. I wish to state at the outset that my decision in the *Hong Kong Standard* case not to prosecute Aw Sian was made on the basis that there was inadequate evidence.
>
> I also considered the matter from the public interest angle...
>
> At no point was any consideration given to the political or personal status of Aw Sian...
>
> Under Article 63 of the Basic Law, the Department of Justice shall control criminal prosecutions free from any interference. As Secretary for Justice, I have exercised this independent prerogative impartially in this particular case (*Leung*, South China Morning Post, 5th February 1999).

Leung's statement contained a number of important points and information. She revealed that there were 53 witnesses and nearly 3,000 pages of exhibits in court to prove that the accused were guilty of the offences for which they were prosecuted, but none implicated Aw.

In the course of her statement, Leung refuted allegations that she had no intention of providing an explanation and gave reasons for the delay in agreeing to speak before the legislative panel. She also cited a justice department policy of not disclosing the reasons for "deciding not to prosecute" and the matter being "subjudice" to support her position at that time. Leung dealt at length with the policy for prosecution and tried to convince the panel of her decision. Selected excerpts from her speech help to shed light on her strategy for managing the crisis.

> "...When I made a decision not to prosecute Aw Sian in last year, I found the evidence against the three accused overwhelmingly more weighty than that against Aw Sian....
>
> ...There were no documents or business records that showed any connection between the crimes and Aw Sian....
>
> ...In her statement, Aw Sian repeatedly emphasized that she had no intention to defraud ABC [Audit Bureau of Circulation], that she agreed to increase the printing and sales of the paper to attract advertisers, but she did not know about the details....
>
> ...Ms. Aw did not know about Mornstar [a company set up to absorb the excess newspapers] and was not aware of the falsification of documents. When the ICAC told her what had been done, she said that she had no idea that it constituted false accounting, and insisted that had she known that it

would be necessary to make false accounts, she would not have permitted them to do it. When the ICAC told her of the illegal acts, she immediately told the others to stop. Ms. Aw should perhaps have exercised greater supervision and control of her subordinates. She was perhaps unwise in going along with what she called a temporary plan to assist sales of the paper without going into details as to what was planned. However, I was considering a charge of conspiracy to defraud. I was not convinced that the conduct of Ms. Aw was in fact fraudulent....

...Some people are of the view that since Ms. Aw stood to benefit from the crime, she must be aware of it and be responsible for it. The crime of conspiracy requires an agreement between two or more persons to commit an unlawful act with the intention of carrying it out. There must be an intention to carry out the illegal elements in the conduct contemplated by the agreement, in the knowledge of those facts which rendered the conduct illegal....

...As the evidence against Ms. Aw did not satisfy these criteria, even when taken at its highest, I was not prepared to proceed upon the basis of surmise....

...Since I have concluded that there was no reasonable prospect of securing a conviction, it would be wrong in principle for me to bring a prosecution. Nor will I do so simply to avoid public criticism of my decision....

...Also from the public interest point of view, I considered it not right to prosecute Aw Sian. At that time, the Sing Tao Group was facing financial difficulties and was negotiating restructuring with banks. If Aw Sian was prosecuted, it would be a serious obstacle for restructuring. If the group should collapse, its newspapers (which include one of only two English newspapers in Hong Kong) would be compelled to cease operation. I wish to add that several other newspapers had folded in late 1996, 1997 and 1998. Apart from the staff losing employment, the failure of a well-established important media group at that time could have sent a very bad message to the international community....

...Having assessed the evidence before me and, weighing the effect of the prosecution, the role played by Aw Sian in the matter, and whether the consequences of the prosecution were proportionate to the seriousness of the alleged offense, I decided that Aw Sian should not be prosecuted both from the sufficiency of evidence angle and as a matter of public interest.

...the decision not to prosecute Aw Sian was definitely not a decision made in bad faith....

...As Secretary for Justice, my role is to defend the independence and impartiality of criminal prosecutions. I will not be swayed by public comment to depart from the principles of our prosecution policy. In preserving the rule of law in Hong Kong, I shall adhere to this principle" (*South China Morning Post*, 5th February 1999).

The statement made by the Secretary for Justice turned out to be more a defence of Aw and her actions than what it was intended to be - a defence of the rule of law. It was hardly adequate in convincing the legislators and the public, and could not provide reassurance about the rule of law in Hong Kong. Some of the reasons presented in the statement were rejected outright, as seen from the reaction, which was quick and strong.

Reactions to Leung's Statement

Ronald Arculli of the Liberal Party inquired about the Secretary for Justice's manner of evaluating the case. According to Paragraph 16 of the *Booklet of Prosecution Policy*, it is specified that: "Having satisfied himself that the evidence itself can justify proceedings in the sense that there is a reasonable prospect of obtaining a conviction, Government Counsel must then consider whether the public interest requires a prosecution". In view of this policy, he doubted whether it was necessary for the Secretary for Justice to have considered the public interest at all, since insufficient evidence prevented a conviction against Sally Aw.

Albert Ho of the Democratic Party, on the other hand, brought forward a pertinent point. He reminded those concerned that the issue of public interest had to be defined with utmost care, and he was concerned that the Secretary for Justice had employed an incorrect definition. Leung's argument carried grave implications that could possibly mislead the public to believe that those that employed large numbers of people could escape the justice of law. Ho's statement brought to the fore the evasive manner in which the statement was presented to the panel.

The Secretary for Justice quoted Paragraph 10 of the *Booklet of Prosecution Policy*, which sets out the relevant factors in the consideration of public interest, and pointed out that it was necessary to consider the implications of how a decision to launch a prosecution would affect "other people". Martin Lee, Chairperson of the Democratic Party, pointed out that "other people" in this case should refer to those who were either directly or indirectly connected to a crime, such as a victim, not employees who were in no way related to the case. Hence, the decision not to prosecute on the basis of the ability of an individual to provide employment to a large number of people pointed toward discrimination in the application of the law.

Bob Broadfoot, Managing Director of a private firm - the Political and Economic Risk Consultancy - commented: "I don't think the decision by the Secretary for Justice marks the end of the integrity of the legal system by any means. The legal system didn't decide not to prosecute Sally Aw, one person decided that. The system wasn't allowed to do its job" (Granitsas, *Far Eastern Economic Review,* 18th February 1999). Broadfoot's view thus led weight to the debate raging over the ability and competence of Leung to serve as the Secretary for Justice. It also opened up discussion on the role expected of such a position.

A related, but slightly different view, was taken by a number of academics. They suggested that the problem rested with the nature of the role of the Secretary for Justice, and not the Secretary for Justice herself. Ghai wrote:

> "If the Secretary for Justice is a key member of the government, running a large department with the responsibility to look after the legal affairs of the administration, it may be hard to divorce prosecution decisions from the politics of government — and even harder to dispel public impression that prosecution decisions are so influenced" (Lau, *South China Morning Post,* 26th March 1998).

It was pointed out that as an appointed civil servant of the government, the Secretary for Justice played the role of both the government's legal adviser and the public prosecution authority. Thus, it was a simple problem because the role was essentially political, and that could be identified as the source of the problems. The two roles came into conflict in sensitive cases such as this and Leung's background, in particular, made the case extra controversial.

The only solution, as suggested by C.K. Lau, was that the "dual roles held by the Secretary for Justice" be separated. Such a move would not be completely unprecedented. Lau pointed out that a number of former British colonies, perhaps out of foresight, had already implemented the changes necessary in their systems to deal with such circumstances. "As the legal system is an important pillar of Hong Kong's success", Lau encouraged the government to "consider adopting such a proposal to ensure prosecution decisions are seen to be free from political interference" (Lau, *South China Morning Post,* 26th March 1998). In fact, perceived interference from political quarters had been posing problems to the Hong Kong Government in the early years after the reversal of sovereignty to China. These were disturbing signs, as attention of the international community remained riveted on Hong Kong to assess the extent of autonomy allowed to this region by the central leadership of the People's Republic of China. Another debate erupted around the same time with the legislation of the Personal Data (Privacy) Ordinance and contributed to further speculation about the effectiveness of rule of law in Hong Kong.

The Xinhua Incident

In February 1998, another case of non-prosecution took place. The information gathering section of the Central Government of the People's Republic of China in Hong Kong, Xinhua News Agency, was exempted from prosecution for the contravention of the Personal Data (Privacy) Ordinance. This move by the government added fuel to suspicions already lurking in the minds of the public. A powerful institution was found to be accorded preferential treatment and the rule of law was apparently rendered ineffective.

The Personal Data (Privacy) Ordinance came into effect on 20th December 1996. Citing the privilege offered by the Ordinance, a sitting member of the Legislative Council, Emily Lau Wai-hing, requested from Xinhua any information that they might have on her. Eleven months later, the news agency followed up Lau's request with a one-lined answer that they had no such file, and in doing so they had breached the 40-day deadline in which they were required to reply. In late February, the Privacy Commissioner, Stephen Lau Ka-men announced that "[Xinhua] breached the provisions of the ordinance and that is an offence" (Manuel, *South China Morning Post,* 28th February 1998).

However, The Department of Justice, after reviewing the complaint, disagreed with the need to prosecute. An explanation for such a decision was refused: "[an explanation] would unfairly reveal that someone had been under suspicion for having committed a criminal offence… to give reasons in public for not prosecuting any person can lead to public debate about the case and about the person's guilt or innocence. That is undesirable and unfair to the person concerned" (Manuel, *South China Morning Post,* 28th February 1998). The explanations, for obvious reasons as well as for the weakness of those given, hardly helped in restoring confidence in the rule of law in Hong Kong.

The Chairman of the Democratic Party, Martin Lee Chu-ming, protested the ruling. He remarked: "Here you have the clearest possible breaches of the law and yet the offender is not prosecuted. And there can only be one reason for that because it is Xinhua". Lee added: "If it were an embassy, a consulate, then of course you are exempted…but Xinhua just calls itself a news agency", and "It has to obey the law" (Humphrey, *Reuters News Service,* 12th March 1998).

At a press conference in Europe, the Chief Executive, Tung Chee-hwa commented that, the case was one of "technical violations, not a substantive breach" (Manuel, *South China Morning Post,* 29th March 1998*)*. But other expressions of concern followed. Legislator Christine Loh wrote, "This was a disturbing response, as it showed a lack of understanding for the rule of law" (1998). "In any event", she continued, "the decision whether to prosecute lies exclusively with the Secretary of Justice, but Tung's comment gave the impression that he had a hand in the decision as well". The Chief Executive's effort to rationalise the decision with legal technicalities did not succeed in satisfying the public.

The issue of the non-prosecution of Xinhua News Agency was eventually lost in the clutter of daily current events, but confidence in Leung's administration of justice and the government's respect for the rule of law had been greatly damaged. It was obvious that different standards were being applied to cases, depending on the standing and position of the parties, and even strong expression of disapproval from the media, the public and legislators was not having any impact. Thus, there was debate over whether the Xinhua News Agency should be extended exemption.

Extending Exemption to the "State"

In fact, at the final sitting of the Beijing-appointed Provisional Legislative Council, in late April 1998, legislators passed amendments to the Adaptation of Laws (Interpretive Provisions) Bill exempting authorities and their subordinate organs from some local laws retrospective to 1 July 1997. The affected ordinances include the Privacy Ordinance, the Sex Discrimination Ordinance, the Occupational Safety and Health Ordinance, Arbitration Ordinance and the Environmental Impact Assessment Ordinance. The government claimed the change to be merely "technical" replacing the British "Crown", exempt from some local laws, to the "State", referring to the Chinese "State". But the public saw it otherwise.

The amendment legalised Xinhua's non-observance of the Privacy Ordinance that occurred when Emily Lau Wai-hing received an overdue reply to her request for information that they would have on her. But most significantly, the amended law blurred the definition of Chinese-run entities. "Once we accept this, it might open a whole box of strange creatures", warned Law Yuk Kai, Director of Hong Kong Human Rights Monitor (Templeman & Einhorn, *Businessweek,* 20th April 1998).

The Chinese government and the People's Liberation Army had many business interests in Hong Kong. "State entities involved in commercial operations are supposedly still subject to Hong Kong laws. But companies could easily dodge that proviso by forming subsidiaries that claim to be state agencies" (Templeman & Einhorn, *Businessweek,* 20th April 1998). *The Asian Wall Street Journal* was wary that such a change in law would put investors at risk: "mainland 'red chip' companies could someday find that there is no way to take a business dispute to court if a company can claim that its connections to the Chinese state render it untouchable" (*The Asian Wall Street Journal*, 9th April 1998).

A debate ensued over whether the amendment was constitutionally sound. According to the Basic Law, Chinese government offices, including the Peoples' Liberation Army, were required to "abide by the laws of the region". The Secretary for Justice defended the new amendment by saying that it maintained the situation as it was under British rule. Ghai refuted Leung's defence and said that the transfer of the Crown's old privileges to the Chinese state was based on the "mistaken assumption that Hong Kong is a colony of China". After the handover, Hong Kong operated under the 'one country, two systems' principle, giving it considerable autonomy from the Chinese government. Leung's argument was unsound, again bringing into doubt her judicial independence. The level of concern was heightened as another case related to the right of abode indicated.

Another Case: the Authority of the Court of Final Appeal

Shortly after the reversal of sovereignty to China, Hong Kong's judicial system had to face a controversial case relating to the right of abode of a group of children. Uncertainty prevailed over the residence status of children whose parents were not permanent residents of Hong Kong when the children were born. Although the parents attained permanent residence subsequently, this privilege was not automatically granted to the children, who were liable to be deported from Hong Kong at any time and thus ran the risk of being separated from their parents.

At the heart of the constitutional dispute were several mainland children who appealed to the court saying they had the right of abode in Hong Kong under the Basic Law, because they had at least one parent who was a Hong Kong permanent resident. The court ruled in their favour and, in narrowing the scope for referring such cases to the National People's Congress, it claimed primary jurisdiction in the territory. On 29th January

1999, the Court of Final Appeal ruled that the immigration laws formulated in July 1998 could not be made retrospective, allowed the children from the People's republic of China to continue residing in Hong Kong, and more significantly, gave the courts of Hong Kong power to interfere in NPC decisions which contravened the Basic Law.

Hong Kong's Court of Final Appeal claimed that the local courts had the right to determine "whether an act of the National People's Congress or its Standing Committee is inconsistent with the Basic Law". If it was, the court insisted, it could declare their application in Hong Kong invalid.

The verdict of the Court of Final Appeal was appreciated by legal experts, politicians, and the business community in Hong Kong, and was viewed as a resounding victory for the rule of law. However, four mainland legal experts described the court ruling on right of abode as a challenge to the NPC. The experts, all former Basic Law drafters, said the landmark ruling was an attempt by the Court of Final Appeal to extend its jurisdiction to Beijing and turn Hong Kong into an independent political entity. It also violated the Basic Law. Zhao Qizheng of the State Council remarked that "[t]hey [the mainland experts] are not in contradiction with the government view. At an appropriate time, the Government will express its opinion. The court decision is a mistake and against the Basic Law; the Basic Law cannot be changed. The court decision should be changed" (O'Neill, 9th February 1999, *South China Morning Post*). Thus, the ruling was denounced by legal experts and the press in China as an attack on China's sovereignty.

Hong Kong politicians and the local bar association defended the court by saying that it had merely put the rule of law above the power of the National People's Congress (NPC). This went against the nature of the Chinese system, where the NPC takes precedence on such matters. On notions such as judicial review, Hong Kong's legal profession is steeped in a common law tradition, while China's legal experts believe the NPC has absolute authority. The Chief Executive of Hong Kong successfully solicited the assistance of the Standing Committee of the NPC to reverse the ruling of the Court of Final Appeal. Not only did it reduce the dignity and status of the court, but it also gave rise to doubts about the guarantee of Hong Kong's autonomy and the rights of its residents elaborated in the Joint Declaration and entrenched in the Basic Law. The attacks on the judiciary that accompanied these moves affected its morale. Certainly, they compelled a grafting of mainland law on Hong Kong, undermining its common-law foundation (Ghai, *Far Eastern Economic Review,* 13th January 2000).

Since that verdict was generally welcomed in Hong Kong, the official reaction from Beijing only succeeded in raising questions about the practical workings of the "one country, two systems" principle. China's central government felt that the decision was simply impractical at a time of rising unemployment, and some officials were concerned that it could lead to an increase in illegal immigration. Aside from practical considerations, it shows the vast difference between Hong Kong and China in matters relating to the concept of the law. Despite the advances made towards rule by law in China, official interpretation still goes through a prism of politics and practicality (*South China Morning Post*, 9th February 1999). In Hong Kong, on the other hand, the supremacy and independence of the Common Law is an essential element in the system that has run through the handover.

The Secretary for Justice met the mainland legal experts to discuss the constitutional crisis. She said the views of Hong Kong people, including the legal sector, had been reflected but "my intention…is not to alter the views of anybody" (Hon, *South China Morning Post*, 12th February 1999). Later, the Secretary for Justice announced that the Central government believed part of the Court of Final Appeal's judgement on the right of abode breached the constitution and the Basic law and needed to be rectified. This episode in the legal history of Hong Kong further affected dwindling public confidence in the rule of law.

Issues and Lessons

The rule of law constitutes an essential element of governing modern states. It is critical in ensuring the functioning of the system and instils a sense of confidence among citizens. They are assured that the polity is run on the basis of a set of rules that are applied neutrally and impartially. In this, every citizen feels secure and is protected from unjust persecution. One of the most important tasks of public management is to ensure that the rule of law is upheld at all times. In Hong Kong, the case of the non-prosecution of the owner of the *Hong Kong Standard* newspaper, an influential and wealthy businessperson, seemed to indicate that it does not operate in the territory.

In view of such a situation, the first task of public managers would be to ensure the effective operation of the rule of law. It was necessary to present information and evidence to restore the public's confidence in the system. Instead of adopting such an approach, the government pursued an evasive strategy by stating that the reasons for the non-prosecution of alleged conspirators was not disclosed. This did not serve as an effective explanation. The Secretary for Justice cited several other cases in which decisions for non-prosecution were made, but that statement did not have an impact on the perception of the citizens about the rule of law.

Under pressure from legislators, the media and the public, the Secretary for Justice eventually took steps to provide information on the case. In a long and rambling statement, she sought to defend her decision not to prosecute. In the process, she made further blunders by referring to the ability of Aw to employ a large number of people as a factor considered in reaching the decision. This actually confirmed the public's apprehension that an affluent businessperson was exempted from prosecution due to her wealth and position in society.

The Secretary for Justice's performance during this period revealed a number of weaknesses in her personality and gave rise to questions about her ability to serve in such an important position. Her handling of the case was explained with reference to her lack of experience in criminal prosecutions. Her inability to follow procedures and seek opinions from the appropriate counsels suggested that this important position was held by a person with inadequate qualifications and experience. There were indications that the Secretary for Justice was finding it difficult to justify the legal decisions and present facts convincingly to the public and legislators. Above all, she was unable to prosecute a person who was named as a co-conspirator in a case of perpetuating fraud.

The most important lesson from this case is that the rule of law should be faithfully followed, and prosecution should be initiated in accordance with the charges filed. The courts should be allowed to establish the guilt or innocence of an accused, and this would establish the effectiveness of rule of law. The independence of the courts must be upheld, and public managers have to make efforts to assist the judiciary in performing its duties.

This case, similar to most of the others, suggests the importance of transparency in managing crises in public organisations. The public's confidence in the rule of law declined as there was pre-existing apprehension over the willingness of the People's Republic of China to allow Hong Kong to function independent of any influence. The decision not to prosecute a person perceived to have close ties with the Chief Executive served to reinforce such a conception. The crisis worsened as the government chose a strategy of evasiveness instead of transparency. A free and open discussion of the issues involved in the case and an effective presentation of the facts to the public and their representatives in the Legislative Council could have diffused much of the anxiety resulting from the case.

The final issue in the case stems from the perceived capability of senior public officials. Although in cases of crises in public management in Hong Kong, the credibility of several senior public managers was brought into question, the Secretary for Justice received particularly harsh treatment. Her style may have been influenced by her lack of experience in public service. But it is more likely that the crisis faced by her department was related to a fundamental area of concern to which the future of Hong Kong is intimately linked.

5 Managing Public Infrastructure

With the expansion of the functions and responsibilities of governments over the years, public infrastructure has assumed an increased importance in the field of public management. On the one hand, the planning and construction of infrastructure involves consideration of the needs, the capabilities and the eventual benefits to be obtained from such facilities. On the other hand, major physical infrastructure requires huge resources. Since these projects are mostly financed through the public exchequer, their management also involves a number of technical functions including invitation, award, and the management of contracts. Efforts are made to ensure that the projects are completed within planned time frames, are of acceptable standards and quality, and that they are ready for providing the service expected.

The management of public infrastructure, particularly at the planning and construction stage, is becoming increasingly complex. "Major decisions related to the construction of facilities, their location, the amount of resources to be allocated for this purpose, as well as the assessment of their impact on the physical, economic and social environment have to be carefully considered" (Huque, 1997, p. 5). Hong Kong's most prestigious project, the construction of a new airport, started off among mixed concerns. At the early stages of planning, there were some concerns about the feasibility and implementation of the project, but subsequently expectations were raised with constant assurances and statements from the government.

This case explores the problems encountered on the opening day of the new Hong Kong International Airport. With the resources and effort invested in the project, it was expected to proceed very smoothly from the construction to the operational stage. Unfortunately, a number of malfunctions were evident on the first day, and speculations abound on the causes of such failures. On the surface, the problems were not of a critical nature - the flight display boards and the baggage handling systems malfunctioned. However, the cost could have been much higher had a major accident taken place. Nevertheless, the cost in terms of damage to the reputation of the otherwise efficient Hong Kong government was considerable.

The Case

Hong Kong's Kai Tak Airport had served the territory extremely well for a number of years, but it was operating well beyond capacity during the period leading up to the reversal of sovereignty. The volume of air traffic had increased manifold, and the hugely enhanced volume of cargo handled made a new airport a necessity, since there was no room for expansion at the existing location.

There were many additional benefits to be achieved from a new airport. It would provide Hong Kong with a competitive edge as a travel hub in the region, boost the economy and restore confidence in the future of territory. Therefore, when David Wilson, then Governor of Hong Kong, announced in 1989 plans for a new airport, in an attempt to rebuild confidence in Hong Kong after the Tiananmen Square incident, the initial reaction was both of excitement and exasperation. To Hong Kong citizens, the thought of building Asia's largest and most modern airport boosted optimism and hope. Even those who were originally displeased by the proposal, such as senior public officials from Beijing who were closely involved in the Sino-British negotiations, eventually appeared to be impressed by the plan.

The huge magnitude of the project called for the establishment of an appropriate management framework. Since the new airport was to be a public infrastructure project, the Works Department (Works Bureau since 1 July 1997) had to be closely involved. However, it also meant numerous contracts and sub-contracts had to be awarded and monitored. The Provisional Airport Authority was set up in 1990 for implementing the project, and in December 1995, the Airport Authority Ordinance established the Airport Authority (AA) as a statutory body. Managed by a Board of fifteen members, it had the mandate of developing and operating the airport as a commercial entity. In addition to nine non-official members, the board included six ex-officio members - Secretary for Economic Services, Secretary for the Treasury, Secretary for Works, Director of Civil Aviation, Chief Executive of the Hong Kong Monetary Authority, and the Director of NAPCO (New Airport Projects Co-ordination Office). Its Chief Executive Officer, who had 1,800 staff at his disposal, headed the management of the AA. AA management was responsible for the operation of the new airport, and its board received regular reports on the progress of work from the management.

The Airport Development Steering Committee (ADSCOM) was chaired by the Chief Secretary and included the Financial Secretary, Secretary for Economic Services, Secretary for Planning, Environment and Lands, Secretary for the Treasury, Secretary for Transport, and the Secretary for Works as members. This body had the responsibility of establishing policy, guiding the implementation of the Airport Core Project, monitoring progress by receiving reports from the AA, and generally to "provide an overall steer on issues with significant policy or resources implications" (*Commission of Inquiry* 1999, Paras 5.22-5.24).

NAPCO consisted of a Project Management Office, the Media Relations and the Community Relations Division, the Committee Secretariat, Administration and Support Division, and the Legal Advisory Division. Its main task was to co-ordinate the ten core airport projects, and in addition manage project implementation, and co-ordinate the government's public information and community involvement programmes (Office of the Ombudsman 1999, p. 19).

Thus, a complex set up of agencies, organisations and personalities - both from the public as well as private sectors - was put in place to guide and implement this major project. It is understandable that such arrangements could lead to a breakdown in communications and affect the effective co-ordination of tasks. It was not unusual to find overlapping responsibilities and jurisdictional vagueness that could contribute to a misunderstanding of the role of the various agencies involved. The establishment of several new bodies reflected the government's eagerness to plan and proceed with the project in a well co-ordinated manner, but the events on the opening day indicated that the approach did not yield the desired result.

Two years after its chaotic opening, the new airport has eventually met the expectations of the public. Situated at Chek Lap Kok in northern Lantau Island, it covers an enormous 1248 hectares; three times the size of the old Kai Tak Airport in Kowloon. A complicated synchronisation of roads, ferries, bridges and light rail, transport the expected 35 million passengers and three million tonnes of cargo a year between Lantau Island and the main urban areas of Hong Kong. At the onset of the Asian financial crisis in 1997, as Hong Kong slipped deeper into recession, expectation for the airport peaked. Correspondents for an international magazine, Barbara Koh and Anastasia Stanmeyer, appropriately captured the sentiments of the public: "The new airport symbolizes everything the glittering city aspires to be. It is grand enough to serve as the major regional hub, not just a way station in southern China. For that matter, it will rank as the finest facility in all of China far into the future—a suitable emblem of china's richest city. It will be efficient, practical and high-tech, just the way Hong Kong sees its own character" (Koh & Stanmeyer, *Newsweek*, 13th July 1998).

From the beginning however, the airport project was plagued with problem after problem, threatening its timely completion. In the beginning, years of tense Sino-British relations hindered adequate progress. A breakthrough was expected with British Prime Minister, John Major's, 1991 visit to the Mainland for the signing of the Memorandum of Understanding on the airport between the two countries. Not long thereafter, however, the airport again became an area of disagreement. Patten's first policy address in 1992 lamented on the possibility that as a consequence of "timetable slips" and "the costs rise", he would "have to fly out of Kai Tak or leave on the *Lady Maurine*" at the handover (Policy Address, 1992). His speech foreshadowed the developments of the Chek Lap Kok project. Disagreements between the British and the Chinese were eventually conciliated to a workable degree, but delays remained the main issue of conflict between stakeholders within Hong Kong throughout the rest of the following six years. Delays would never be fully addressed, leading to imminent crisis on 6th July 1998 when Chek Lap Kok opened to the public for the first time. Additionally, a number of factors that contributed to the escalation of the crisis can be identified.

The Opening Date

The date of the airport's grand opening was a highly politicised issue in pre-handover Hong Kong. As in the case of many of their major infrastructure projects, such as the Strategic Sewage Disposal Scheme, the British were convinced that completion before the handover was of paramount importance. Although this was never mentioned publicly, it seemed to be an appropriate way to end the colonial legacy. China, on the other hand, saw this as an effort to drain resources from the coffers of Hong Kong and was intensely irritated by British efforts to accelerate major engineering works. Friction surrounding the airport inevitably subsided when, to China's delight, it became evident that the project could not in any way be completed before the handover. At the Financial Support Agreement reached between the British and the Chinese on 30th June 1995, the target opening date for the airport was extended to April 1998.

Even after this deadline extension, it seemed highly improbable that the airport would be completed on time. The Airport Authority, the executive body responsible for its operational readiness, faced two issues that sparked debate regarding the opening date. Firstly, Hong Kong Air Cargo Terminals Limited (HACTL), which was in charge of SuperTerminal 1, a large part of the Airport Core Project, were concerned that they would not be able to operate at a sufficient level by April 1998. Secondly, the rail link to the airport was not scheduled to be completed until June of that year.

One of the most essential parts of the Airport Core Project was SuperTerminal 1, the brainchild of HACTL, Hong Kong's largest air cargo handler. Designed to handle 2.5 million tonnes a year, it would become the largest single cargo terminal in the world. Complex software would automate cargo handling and increase the maximum load capacity to almost double that handled at Kai Tak. As early as 1996, however, Anthony Charter, the Managing Director of HACTL, was certain that construction problems upsetting the progress of the airport required a re-evaluation of the opening date. By June 1997, he was aggressively lobbying the government to conduct a full risk analysis to determine a realistic date. Charter said, "For us to be ready at the beginning of April would require substantial acceleration (in the terminal construction project), and we're not sure how achievable it might be" (Tabakoff, *South China Morning Post,* 17th June 1997). By November 1997, SuperTerminal 1 was forecast to be functioning at only about 50 percent of maximum cargo capacity by the April opening date. In response to the prediction, the AA quickly stated that this would be sufficient for the opening date, alleviating concerns raised earlier by Anthony Charter that the opening date should be postponed.

Concerns regarding the completion of the Airport Railway, under the management of the Mass Transit Railway Corporation (MTRC), however, remained. Estimated to carry 40 percent of all passengers to and from the airport, it was scheduled for completion in June 1998. Despite the apparent two-month difference in completion dates, the government was certain the airport could be opened for commercial flights in April for two reasons. First, officials were adamant that the MTRC had a sound record in construction. They maintained that they could speed up the project and shorten its 43 month-long construction period. Secondly, transport officials maintained that the airport could still be operated without a rail link; it was believed that a careful co-ordination of the territories' main public bus operators would facilitate the April opening. This second reason for opening the airport without the railway was abandoned however, as the government began to consider the railway as an integral part of the completed facility.

Thus, it was a major challenge to co-ordinate the completion of HACTL's SuperTerminal 1 and the MTRC's Airport Railway. Nevertheless, the AA, headed by its Chief Executive Henry Townsend, was still certain that Chek Lap Kok would be ready by April 1998. The Director of Corporate Development, Clinton Leeks, the spokesperson for the AA, staunchly stated at every possible opportunity that the April deadline would be met. He said, "Lots of people may not like the dates, but in the end, reality is reality. You can't slow up one of Hong Kong's great economic engines because of one cog" (Tabakoff, *South China Morning Post,* 27th June 1997).

Officials charged with the task of monitoring progress also expressed confidence in the April deadline. Secretary for Economic Services, Stephen Ip Shu-kwan surmised that the airport would be completed on schedule, "[s]o there is no need for contingency plans at the moment" (Tabakoff, *South China Morning Post,* 5th July 1997). At an Economic Services Panel meeting at the Provisional Legislative Council, Ip urged members to have faith in the AA experts, assuring that government bureaus and departments were working closely to ensure the safety of the airport operation at all times (*Minutes of Panel on Economic Services,* 9th March 1998).

The MTRC, on the other hand, did not seem to have that much confidence - neither in the AA nor with the opening date in April. The MTRC had always maintained that it would wait for the AA to prove that it could actually open the airport by April 1998. Until that proof was presented, there were no plans to speed-up construction since there was no guarantee that with accelerated measures the Airport Railway could meet the deadline, let alone do so within budget. It was predicted that any new effort to speed up construction for an April opening would result in a hefty increase of HK$1 billion dollars in their budget. On the other hand, to delay the opening for two months to accommodate the railway would, according to AA Chairman Wong Po-yan, result in economic losses from lost revenue, rent and landing fees.

On January 13th 1998, after considering the case of the MTRC among other matters, the government finally announced that the opening date would be postponed to Monday, 6th July 1998. This allowed for the completion of the Airport Railway in order to have all facilities available for the world class facility. The government was criticised for the delayed announcement, since it had been long clear that the Airport Railway would not meet the previous April deadline. Critics were saying that the government was scared to make anymore hasty decisions in light of its handling of the slaughter of 1.5 millions chickens during the "bird flu" crisis. Although the AA welcomed the decision, they continued to maintain that the airport would nevertheless be ready by April as originally scheduled. Shortly afterwards, Townsend sparked outrage by announcing that the delay of the airport project opening date by nine weeks, from the intended April date, would cost an extra HK$2 billion dollars.

Richard Stirland, Director of the Association of Asia Pacific Airlines, commented on the much-debated opening date in the *South China Morning Post* on 18th January 1998: "From my contacts with the airlines, an April opening would have been feasible but unlikely and quite problematic. People do open airports that are not completely finished. Not having the rail link in place was going to pose a problem for passengers and in turn the airlines. But the major concern was whether the whole automation and information technology side was functioning. If not it could have caused chaos".

High anticipation about the new airport was partially stimulated by the immense campaign that had taken place in drumming up support for this project. Months earlier, the Miss Hong Kong beauty pageant was broadcast from the barely complete main terminal building. The opening ceremony, in partial celebration of the first year of the establishment of the Special Administrative Region, was also held in the halls of the airport. To the delight of all Hong Kong people, both the President of the United States and the President of the People's Republic of China would arrive and depart from the new runway of Chek Lap Kok before any commercial flights would be permitted. It was a sign of confidence from two of the most powerful countries in the world, glorifying Hong Kong for its ingenuity symbolised by the airport.

The Crisis

President Jiang Zhemin of the People's Republic of China officially opened the new airport on 2nd July 1998, and it was opened to commercial air traffic on 6th July. On the first day of operations, the Chief Secretary for Administration and AA executives were able to greet passengers of the first flight, which arrived from New York. Within a few hours, numerous problems were encountered, and the shiny new airport was affected with chaos and confusion. The crisis that followed raised questions and put into doubt the abilities of the management.

Passengers had to compete with sightseers for food and water, which appeared to be inadequate in supply. The principal automated operations such as the luggage handling system, the flight information displays and the air cargo handling services broke down because of software glitches. These problems caused massive chaos. Departing passengers had to wait for hours for their flight to take-off, and those arriving waited similarly for their bags. The opening of Hong Kong's most prestigious infrastructure project turned out to be a major crisis, which would haunt the government for months to come.

A report prepared by the Research and Library Services Division of the Legislative Council Secretariat sought to compile a list of the problems encountered in the passenger terminal building and Airport Railway, by the passengers, in air cargo services, and in the operation of the new airport in general (for details, see Liu, Lee, Wong & Lee, 1998). In the passenger terminal building, air-conditioning units malfunctioned, toilets did not have a water supply, and over 200 public telephones were not connected, while the mobile telephone network did not function. Water and electricity supplies broke down and escalators were not in operation, while passengers had to use emergency exits. The display boards and signposts provided inaccurate information, and the pressroom had only had one telephone installed.

The Airport Railway had its share of problems too. At the airport railway station, ticket machines and turnstiles malfunctioned, and there were complaints about the inappropriate hours during which the service was provided. In addition, there were several other problems with facilities that could be expected to be properly functioning at such an airport.

Passengers were subjected to numerous problems and inconveniences. The "departing passengers were not provided with boarding gate numbers that should normally appear on boarding passes. The airline staff could not help, for they did not have the required information either" (*Report of the Commission of Inquiry*, 1999). Their baggage was misplaced, delayed, missing or undelivered, and some passengers had to wait for more than twenty-four hours for it on the first two days of operation. The computer system broke down which resulted in a chaotic situation. Several flights were delayed due to inadequate supply of fuel, the lack of experience of ramp operators, and lack of co-ordination among the agencies entrusted with the task of their operation. No announcements were made about the delayed flights. The number of shuttle buses was inadequate and passengers had to wait for a long time to board them.

The situation with the air cargo services was equally chaotic. There appeared to be no contingency plan and the entire system was reliant on computers with no manual handling procedures arranged for backup. An unstable electricity supply led to a breakdown of the weighing machines and the disabled computers could not locate cargo. Software and mechanical problems compelled the imposition of a moratorium of all air cargo services.

On the operational side, the ground handling staff were found to be unfamiliar with the facilities at the airport. This was not surprising, since two-thirds of them had little or no experience and had been newly hired for the job. The number of staff operating the airbridges and officers providing information were found to be inadequate.

In addition, the study identified a number of problems encountered in other areas. Trespassers were found in restricted areas, which passengers could leave without clearance from immigration officials. Unaccompanied baggage was found on board, dangerous goods went undetected, and there were communication breakdowns in certain locations. Security appears to have been compromised as no fire drill was reported to have been held in passenger terminals, and fire exits were found to be blocked. Both the fire alarm and sprinkling systems were malfunctioning.

The Commission of Inquiry (1999) listed a total of thirty problems that could be considered to be the cause of the crisis encountered at the new airport:

(1) The unreliable working of FIDS [flight information display systems], with malfunctioning of monitors and LCD [liquid crystal display] boards that were supposed to show flight information
(2) The breakdown of cargo handling by HACTL which eventually imposed an embargo on most import cargo and some export cargo
(3) Delay in flight departure and arrival
(4) Malfunctioning of the Access Control System
(5) Confusion over parking of planes
(6) Malfunctioning of Aircraft Parking Aids
(7) Late arrival of tarmac buses causing delay to disembarkation of passengers
(8) Insufficient passenger steps and miscommunication amongst staff handling the same
(9) Airbridges malfunctioning
(10) Chaos in baggage handling including malfunctioning of monitors and LCD boards in the baggage reclaim area
(11) Public Address System malfunctioning
(12) Airside security risks
(13) Congestion of vehicular traffic and passenger traffic
(14) No tap water in toilet rooms and tenant areas

(15) No flushing water in toilets
(16) Toilets too small
(17) Urinal problems with water flow, infrared sensors and cleanliness
(18) Insufficient air-conditioning in the PTB [Passenger Terminal Building]
(19) Large number of public telephones not working
(20) Mobile phone service not satisfactory
(21) TMR [Trunk Mobile Radios] service not satisfactory
(22) Escalators breaking down repeatedly
(23) Insufficient or ineffective signage
(24) Slippery and reflective floor
(25) Problems with cleanliness and refuse collection
(26) No sufficient water, electricity and staff at restaurants
(27) Insufficient staff canteens
(28) Automated People Mover stoppage
(29) The Airport Express ("AE") ticketing machines malfunctioning
(30) The AE train delay (Para 7.14).

As the inquiry progressed, the commission found further problems that interrupted the operation of the airport. These included the detection of rats, inefficient handling of the needs of an arriving passenger who had suffered a heart attack, failure of emergency services to attend to a worker, fire engines crossing the path of an arriving aircraft, a traffic accident involving a fire engine, a tractor crashing into a light goods vehicle, a power cut trapping passengers in lifts, missed approach by an arriving flight, runway closure following a burst tyre of an aircraft, power outage of SuperTerminal 1, and radio frequency interference on air traffic control frequency (1999, Para 8.1).

Managing the Crisis

The management appeared to have been caught completely off guard by the circumstances. While the confusion continued, some feeble efforts were made to contain the crisis and deal with some of the problems that presented themselves. Subsequent reports from the airport management indicated efforts to manage the crisis. Although the efforts were too little, too late, they indicate the ability to respond to problems in the face of adverse situations.

For example, the cooling system was reported to have been restored and the frequency of cleaning the toilets was increased; the contractor was asked to increase manpower to improve their condition. Similarly, the telephone services were also made operational within a short period of time. The escalators and elevators were brought back to operating condition, and a continuous supply of water and electricity was ensured. The quantity of incorrect information on signboards was ascertained, and temporary signs were installed. The malfunctioning ticketing machines at the airport railway station were repaired and the turnstiles were made operable. After the initial disruption, the waiting time for baggage could be reduced to some extent.

A number of steps were taken to deal with the major problem - the breakdown of the cargo handling system. Flights were diverted to other airports in the region, and temporary arrangements were made to allow some cargo to be exported using the AirFreight Forwarding Centre at the airport. Additionally, the government also offered storage of cargo in the basement at Kai Tak free of charge. The cargo handling capacity of the new airport was gradually enhanced throughout the months of July and August, and full service was achieved by the end of August 1998. It was obvious that problems in certain areas, such as the breakdown of the information system and the operation of air cargo services, were formidable and it was not possible to remedy them immediately. Surprisingly, no immediate attempt was evident to deal with problems related with security.

However, while these steps were being taken to restore a semblance of order at the new airport, the authorities appeared unfazed by the seriousness of the crisis. Making no attempt to recognise the crisis or indicating any intention to deal with it, statements were made that damaged the public's confidence in the ability of the government in managing public services, as well as upholding the value of transparency. Spokesperson for the AA, Clinton Leeks commented: "Without sounding complacent because that's not right, we're fairly satisfied the way things are. I'm not trying to say we're totally satisfied, that would be wrong" (*South China Morning Post*, 7ᵗʰ July 1998).

The Chief Executive made similar reassuring statements. "There are some problems when such a huge airport starts to run. I believe that the Airport Authority will overcome the problems quickly and the airport will operate smoothly", he said. Their remarks sparked off a barrage of criticism from the public. The government, it seemed, was making light on the matter, but days into the crisis, it became clear that the much awaited Chek Lap Kok Airport had become everything Hong Kong feared. In the words of legislator Lau Kong-wah of the Democratic Alliance for the Betterment of Hong Kong, the airport was the "laughing stock of the world" (Hon, *South China Morning Post,* 10ᵗʰ July 1998). There were, in fact, several areas in which crisis erupted on the day of opening, and their causes can be traced back in the history of the construction of the project.

The Cargo Terminal Crisis

In May 1995, the AA, or then the Provisional Airport Authority (PAA), requested of HACTL an opening date of 1st April, 1998. HACTL, even then, stated that such a date would be a rush. Peter Johansen, then the Chairman of HACTL, analysed the situation further; the 3-year time to design, construct, build, maintain and run Super Terminal 1 (ST1) and the software, which is the most complex item, seemed optimistic. Townsend and the rest of the PAA did not accept this, but subsequently a contract between the AA and HACTL stating that ST1 was to be built and run at a 75 percent capacity by 18th August 1998 was signed on 21st December 1995. An informal, "best endeavours" programme was added in August 1996 - to have 50 percent operational capacity of ST1 by April 1998. This would be the foundation of the problems that would later plague HACTL.

The rush for an early opening resulted in software difficulties, training inadequacies and operation problems. Software programmers were constantly rushed to prepare usable software for SuperTerminal 1, and they could not complete ample beta testing for bugs and application problems. Employees using the application were not yet fully trained in using the software, hardware, and equipment to process the cargo. Building delays led to operator problems that started with the fact that ST1 has multiple loading stations and Kai Tak had only one. Communication problems and the use of manual inventory management created massive confusion. These problems gave way to the container traffic jams that ultimately led to the breakdown.

Another problem with regard to the ability and readiness of the personnel can be identified. Apparently, the management of the airport provided practically no facilities for the employees to prepare to do their job. It is quite possible that in order to meet the advanced opening deadline, employees had to be recruited in a hurry and were not provided with the required amount of training. Consequently, they were unable to perform at the required standard. They were forced to improvise and therefore lost control of the situation that arose.

A third problem stemmed from the lack of attention to warnings and commitments by the management and co-ordinators of the project. These informal "programs" resulted in a loss of control and responsibility, lost warnings, unrealistic commitments and confusion. HACTL was not formally responsible for an April 1998 opening. Therefore, it was committed to the "best endeavours" program, when there was no real ability or obligation to actually facilitate such an arrangement. Thus, when the head of HACTL warned the Chief Secretary that there would be a large risk involved with opening in April 1998, neither party were regarding the issue as a serious threat. This indicates another problem in the area of accountability.

Yet another problem was related to the fact that the eyes of the public were riveted on this prestigious project. As HACTL, AA and the Legislative Council tried to find the persons responsible, they were presented with arguments, counter-arguments and confusion. It seemed inconceivable that so many things could go wrong at the same time in such a project, and all the stakeholders appeared determined to pinpoint responsibility. Pressure from the public, the private sector, from the media and different government agencies increased the finger pointing, which ultimately did not prove to be productive.

The Immediate Impact

The public was disconcerted by the chaos, and a large number of people rushed to the airport to view the situation, which further intensified the disorder. Members of the legislature were dissatisfied with the outcome, and some speculated that the opening date might have been brought forward to coincide with the first anniversary of the handover and the visits by President Jiang Zemin and President Bill Clinton. Others speculated that corruption had been involved, since days before the opening a number of persons were charged by the Independent Commission Against Corruption (ICAC), regarding piling problems with some of the buildings at the airport and a number of airport rail stations. Meanwhile, the Chairman of the Authority, Wong Po-yan and the Deputy Chief Executive, Billy La Chun-lung, apologised for the airport chaos, and expressed regret and shame over the incident.

Urgent ad hoc talks and meetings were held within the government to deal with the crisis. On 10th July 1998, the Chief Secretary for Administration announced that the Chief Executive, Tung Chee-hwa, had decided to appoint an independent commission into the airport chaos, which would include experts and leading members of the community. Membership of the commission was to be announced at a later date. In this regard, Tung said: "We must find out why so many problems have cropped up after the airport opening and whose responsibility it is" (Cheung & Ku, *South China Morning Post*, 11ᵗʰ July 1998).

However, legislators were not entirely sure that the investigation would be impartial, since the government would be appointing the investigators. They, therefore, suggested that a select committee be set up to conduct another investigation into matters concerning the airport crisis, should the government probe produce unsatisfactory results. The Chief Secretary angrily responded to such a notion: "I am somewhat surprised that some members should have called into question the integrity of the investigation even before the team has commenced its work" (Cheung & Ku, *South China Morning Post*, 11ᵗʰ July 1998). Legislators decided that they would first await the outcome of the government investigation and wait no more than three months for the team to complete and submit their report to the Chief Executive. Days later, the Ombudsman announced that he, too, would be conducting an investigation into the crisis, sparking Executive Committee member Chung Sze-yuen to express concern that there would be a duplication of work with three separate but similar investigations.

Meanwhile, the local media undertook their own examination of the top officials of the various agencies involved with the preparations of the airport opening day. The Chief Executive of the AA, Henry Townsend, received the most criticism from this source. It was reported that he had no previous experience in airport management and that his management style played top executives against each other, almost in competition, without any effort for co-ordination (Gittings, *South China Morning Post*, 19ᵗʰ July 1998). It was well known that the government had searched for a replacement for Townsend when his contract needed to be renewed in November 1997. However, none was found, and in November 1998 Townsend was granted a $2.5 million gratuity. This revelation enraged the public.

Public resentment was further heightened since, at about the same time, Wong Po-yan, Chairman of the AA was awarded the Grand Bauhinia Medal. This is the highest public honour that can be bestowed upon a citizen of the Hong Kong Special Administrative Region of the People's Republic of China. In presenting the medal to Wong, the Chief Executive cited Wong's "outstanding contribution to the development of the Hong Kong International Airport at Chek Lap Kok" (*South China Morning Post*, 7ᵗʰ October 1998). The public was hardly impressed with such a claim.

On 20ᵗʰ July, the Chief Executive made his first visit to the airport. Demonstrators were waiting for his arrival, and shouted slogans such as, "Chief Executive loses face over the chaos at the airport" (Lee and Yeung, *South China Morning Post*, 21ˢᵗ July 1998). The public was so outraged that it took the Chief Executive two weeks before he was able to visit the crisis area. In response he said, "I have not come to the airport because my colleague, Mrs. Chan [the Chief secretary for Administration] has been obviously very involved – so have other senior colleagues" (Lee and Yeung, *South China Morning Post,* 21st July 1998). In his typical manner, the Chief Executive managed to say nothing significant, but simply demonstrated his complete reliance on senior public officials to deal with crises. The lack of political direction in managing crises has been a recurrent problem in post-1997 Hong Kong.

Investigating the Crisis

The government's earlier plan regarding its intention to appoint outside experts to the commission for investigation was soon discarded. On 21st July 1998, the government announced the appointment of Mr. Justice Woo Kwok-hing and Dr. Edgar Cheng as heads of the government investigation. This was an interesting development, considering the reservation expressed by some members of the Legislative Council about those appointed by the government. The Chief Executive sought to assure the community, without really achieving that effect by saying, "After much consideration, we think this is a good arrangement" (Yeung, *South China Morning Post,* 22nd July 1998). Woo, a barrister before being appointed to High Court in 1992, was also the Electoral Affairs Commissioner for the first post-handover Legislative Council elections. He had previously overseen an inquiry into the case of a major fire that swept through a building in a densely populated area of Hong Kong. Cheng was a businessman, and headed the University Grants Committee. He was also the Vice-Chairman of Hang Seng Bank and the Chairman of Hong Kong Securities.

The investigation got off to a controversial start. At the outset, Woo issued a warning against further public comments on the fiasco since the matter was "sub judice". He claimed that the probe was a judicial proceeding under the Commissions of Inquiry Ordinance and contempt-of-court safeguards would apply to the inquiry as well (*South China Morning Post,* 23rd July 1998). Woo was immediately criticised for his comment. He defended his position by saying that he had no intention of gagging the public or the media, and just wanted to prevent publications that may prejudice the proceedings (*South China Morning Post,* 24th July 1998).

At a Legislative Council meeting on 29th July 1998, legislators debated about the government's investigation. Legislator Lau Kong-wah moved a resolution to immediately appoint a select committee, disregarding their earlier agreement to postpone a Legislative Council investigation for three months. The reasons were given as follows: "Firstly, 'the group appointed by the Chief Executive to inquire into the operation of the new airport' as in the original wording can no longer refer exactly to the Commission of Inquiry just appointed by the Chief Executive in Council. Secondly, the 'three months' as in the original wording is no longer applicable because it is expected that the Commission of Inquiry cannot conclude its investigation and submit a report in three months" (*Minutes of Legislative Council Meeting*, 29th July 1998). The Legislative Council began preparatory work on the Select Committee immediately.

Thus, the crisis of the opening of the new Hong Kong International Airport prompted three different investigations and their terms of reference make interesting comparison. The Commission of Inquiry on the New Airport appointed by the government sought:

(1) To examine the planning and preparation for the opening of the new airport including the adequacy of the communication and co-ordination between all the interested parties.

(2) To examine the decision to open the new airport on 6 July 1998 and the extent to which it was ready to begin operation on that date.

(3) To examine the operation of the new airport since it opened on 6 July 1998 (including but not limited to, the flight information display system, franchised air cargo services, ramp handling and baggage handling and airside security) and to identify the roles of the various parties involved.

(4) To identify problems encountered in the operation of the new airport and to establish the causes and where the responsibility for each of them lies.

(5) To report to the Chief Executive with findings and conclusions within 6 months of the date of appointment or such time as the Chief Executive in Council may allow (Commission of Inquiry, 1999, p. 6).

The Select Committee appointed by the Legislative Council sought to identify specific areas of concern "to inquire into the circumstances leading to the problems surrounding the commencement of the operation of the new Hong Kong International Airport at Chek Lap Kok since 6 July 1998 and related issues" (Report of the Select Committee, Para.2.1).

The terms of reference suggested that the scope of inquiry would cover ten areas of concern:

(1) the choice of 6th July 1998 as the date of commencement of the operation of the new airport; (2) integration, co-ordination and supervision of construction and operation, including contingency plans; (3) infrastructure and facilities; (4) passenger services; (5) air cargo services; (6) security; (7) airport staff performance; (8) noise under the flight paths; (9) responsibilities and liabilities; and (10) overall economic loss to Hong Kong (Report of the Select Committee, Para.2.3).

The investigation by the Ombudsman appeared to focus on the various agencies and boards involved in the process. Accordingly, the terms of reference stated:

> The purpose of the direct investigation is to investigate the actions of the Airport Authority; the Airport Development and Steering Committee (ADSCOM), New Airport Projects Co-ordination Office (NAPCO) and, where necessary, other offices within the Government Secretariat (Ombudsman Report, Para. 1.3).

All three investigations came to an end in early 1999, and their results published. The findings were not surprising and directed attention to problems with the preparation, following procedures and the manner of organising and monitoring the activities of the various agencies involved in the process. The Commission of Inquiry noted problems related to the adequacy of communication and co-ordination. Noting the composition, responsibilities, performance and relationship among the various agencies involved in preparing and operating the airport, the Commission also identified "problems with personalities", and inadequacy of training as the causes of the crisis. The inquiry revealed the lack of a comprehensive system of risk assessment, contingency plans, or adequate testing of the "systems and their operation in an integrated manner" (Para 18.264). Overall, the impression arose that rushing the project to an early date for opening contributed to the crisis.

The Select Committee of the Legislative Council concluded that most of the problems were foreseeable and that the airport was not ready for operation on the opening date. In particular, it was noted that the "two critical items" - the flight information and display system and Hong Kong Air Cargo Terminals Limited - were not ready on the day of opening the airport, and this could not be explained as "teething problems". Furthermore, the Committee concluded that "The key bodies, namely, ADSCOM [Airport Development Steering Committee], AA [Airport

Authority] Board, AA Management, and HACTL, and some of the key persons of these bodies should take varying degrees of responsibilities for the chaos on AOD [airport opening day]" (Legislative Council Select Committee 1999, p. 181).

The third investigation by the Office of the Ombudsman concluded that the chaos was compounded due to the simultaneous malfunctioning of a number of systems on the airport opening day. This report suggested that "the inadequate communications and lack of co-ordination between the AA, airlines' ramp handlers and bus crews" led to the escalation of the problems and that "the baggage problem was a result of inadequate training and familiarization of the BHS [Baggage Handling System] by operators and ramp handlers". Interface problems between airside and landside operations, under estimation of the task of co-ordination by the AA, lack of a contingency plan in case of serious breakdown, the failure to reassess the practicability of the airport opening date, and the absence of a direct channel of communication between the ADSCOM and non-government (unofficial) members of the AA were also cited as contributors to the crisis (Office of the Ombudsman 1999, pp. 68-75).

Issues and Lessons

A number of issues emerge from the case of the new Hong Kong International Airport. At the simplest level, it could have been caused by a case of nervous jitters at the conclusion of a huge infrastructure project. But the careful consideration of the case and the findings of the three investigations point towards several elements of management that could have contributed to the crisis. The three investigations, one led by government-appointed investigators, another by a Legislative Council Select Committee, and a third by the Ombudsman, uncovered flaws in the management of the Airport Core Project by both the Administration and the Airport Authority.

By all accounts, a lack of appropriate planning can be noticed. There were indications of the lack of basic preparation for the opening on the scheduled date. At various stages, there were indications that the opening date was unrealistic and should have been reconsidered. Two critical elements of the new airport - the railway connection and the baggage handling system - were vital to the successful inauguration, and their breakdown discounted all the creditable work by the managers. Even as the crisis struck, inexperienced and inadequately trained front-line workers were left to correct faults and deal with the irate public. A lack of preparation was also revealed during the investigations. Various systems were not properly tested and the shortening of the preparation period probably compelled the management to neglect the establishment of a contingency plan.

Several problems could be detected in the organisational arrangements. Breakdowns in communication and a lack of co-ordination have been highlighted in the reports of the investigators. This could be viewed as the outcome of the establishment of several bodies without clearly defining their roles and responsibilities. The relationships between AA, ADCOM and NAPCO remained vague and complex, particularly some overlapping memberships of senior public officials. While many were included in the membership of the key bodies, the functions expected of them were not sufficiently clarified. The lack of adequate and effective monitoring and supervision of the progress and quality of work has been identified by the investigations. As some members were serving on different committees, the task of monitoring became an even larger challenge as, in some way, they were expected to monitor and supervise their own work.

The leadership of the most senior public official was put under the spotlight during the investigations. While it may be argued that the Chief Secretary for Administration, as the Chairperson of ADSCOM, could be held responsible for the crisis and its ineffective management, the issue revolves around the nature of the relationship between the specialists and generalists. The Chief Secretary was put in charge as a senior public official, but she had to be assisted by specialists who were expected to be familiar with the problems and pitfalls in implementing such a project. Under these circumstances, questions may be raised over the extent of delegation and autonomy enjoyed by the specialists.

This point leads to the consideration of political influence in making decisions relating to public infrastructure. There have been speculations that the opening date of the airport was brought forward under political considerations, to score diplomatic points by synchronising it with the visits by the American and Chinese presidents. If that was the case, then the views of specialists and other members may have not been given adequate importance in revising the date of inauguration. That would indicate a serious lapse of judgement, since it would have meant going ahead, with the expectation that everything would fall into place by 6th July 1998. Such an approach is not consistent with the principles of effective management of public services.

Conjecture over the decision making style also has relevance to the potential problem of personality conflicts. With a collection of extremely competent and powerful personalities from both the public and private sectors, the possibility of conflicts cannot be ruled out. The pattern of thinking of public officials, technical experts and private contractors are likely to reflect different orientations, and each would accord priority to different elements. All these factors could have combined to produce quality decisions, should there have been effective communication and co-ordination. Yet the absence of these facilitating elements produced formidable barriers to the process and consequently resulted in the ineffective management of the crisis when it eventually struck.

Finally, the circumstances also give rise to apprehensions about the possibility of "groupthink" (for details on the concept, see Arnold & Feldman, 1986, pp. 412-13). Decisions in public organisations may be influenced by the presence of powerful protagonists. Under such circumstances, suggestions emanating from powerful sources may not be adequately discussed and debated, as the hierarchical nature of bureaucratic set ups prevents effective two-way communication. Consequently, members of the group making a decision on the opening date for the airport may have mutually reinforced the suggestion and remained oblivious to the pitfalls in its advancement.

Several lessons may be drawn from this case. The most obvious one is that the dates of inaugurating major public facilities should not be rushed as the costs can exceed the benefits by a large margin. It was fortunate that major accidents did not take place on the day the airport was opened, but that possibility could not have been ruled out, as the system was yet to become fully functional.

The Commission of Inquiry emphasised the "fitness of the personality and character of the persons occupying key posts" as well as the "interaction of the personalities of those occupying such posts", "a global and comprehensive risk assessment", and "comprehensive contingency plans to cater for various eventualities..." (1999, Paras. 18.270, 18.272, 18.275).

The Legislative Council Select Committee's list of lessons included giving governing bodies authority commensurate with responsibility; ensuring that the authority of governing bodies is not undermined; appointing competent and committed people to governing bodies of executive authorities; clarifying user requirement at the beginning of a project and entertaining no request for change beyond a point of time; appointing professionals to head monitoring bodies for large infrastructure projects; avoiding the creation of too many committees with overlapping functions and responsibilities in the same organisation; preparing, studying and following up progress reports; documenting decisions in organisations; the management of large-scale and complex projects by personnel with relevant experience; co-ordinating activities of business partners; fixing project completion dates before related contracts are awarded; assessing risk and preparing contingency plans for large-scale or complex operations; recognising the importance of information technology; allowing ample time for testing and commissioning systems involving new and advanced technology; and government recognition of the importance of community consideration in project planning (Legislative Council Select Committee, 1999, pp. 238-48).

While the management of the crisis on the opening date was unimpressive, much of the subsequent discussion and investigations have focused on the construction process and preparatory arrangements. It is admitted that in this case, many of the problems could be related to these factors. However, when the crisis actually erupted, it was possible for the AA to deal with the minor problems, while the major ones required more time. Many of the relatively minor malfunctions and faults were corrected within a short time, and no security risk was apparent. However, the breakdown of the information systems and cargo handling represented a crisis, and subsequent developments underline the importance of monitoring and supervision during the planning and construction of public infrastructure.

6 Crises, Strategies and Lessons

Crises are commonplace in the management of public services. The processes of planning, organising and delivering acceptable quality goods and services to the citizens of modern states are extremely complex and difficult. With the progress of civilisation and the maturation of political systems, the scope and pattern of governmental involvement has expanded to cover a wide range of activities. The tasks performed by public organisations reflect the various roles and responsibilities of modern governments. Baker summarised the tasks performed by managers in the public service, and suggested that they generally involve three kinds of activity:

(a) The maintenance of standard, often repetitive patterns of behaviour and relationships -- regulatory activities which must severely, although not completely, limit the element of discretion.
(b) Adaptive/creative activities -- which adapt policies, laws, rules, regulations and standard patterns of activities to the changing needs of society and create new forms and patterns of activity -- all this largely by the interaction of many individuals and groups within and outside the public administration system.
(c) The managerial activities involved in running a great variety of public services (1972, p. 145).

Traditionally, governments have performed a restrictive role to prevent the occurrence of crimes or acts that are harmful to other members of society. Law and order, customs, and immigration are some examples of such services. A set of laws and rules are used to restrict the actions and behaviour of individuals, groups and organisations to facilitate the operation of society. Governments have to take a stern approach in providing such services, and often face criticism as some groups or citizens may perceive the strict application of rules as persecution.

At the same time, governments also play a facilitating role in assisting citizens to realise their potential in life. Services are devised and offered to citizens to provide opportunities to acquire skills, techniques and other requirements for a productive life. Public services related to

107

education, health, welfare and recreation are among those that contribute to this end. In these areas, the government tries to create, preserve and further structures and operations to allow the public maximum opportunity to achieve their objectives. Due to the limited availability of resources and the high level of demand, there must be adequate provision for achieving the maximum possible output from limited input.

Both are difficult areas to manage. The restrictive functions often require the exercise of force, and are likely to spark off debates over fundamental rights, propriety of procedures, and freedom of expression. Public managers are usually very sensitive in performing such tasks, and justifiably so, since no government is willing to compromise on matters of security or public finance. There may be demands or requests for special treatment by groups or individuals, and pressure exerted upon public managers. Therefore, the organisation responds by devising specific patterns of behaviour and actions in such areas. All cases are dealt with according to standard regulations, and there is no scope for deviation from the established procedures. This helps the government to maintain a neutral image in the eyes of the public, and is considered to be one of the strongest attributes of modern bureaucracies. Similarly, in performing the facilitating role, public managers need another set of criteria to determine eligibility and provide services. Generally, routine procedure and practices influence and guide public managers' pattern of behaviour and decision processes.

However, the real test of the structures and personnel arises when non-routine decisions have to be made. This could be the result of changing circumstances, a sudden fall in income or manpower shortage, or a drastic turn of events. Such circumstances leave the officials searching for ways to deal with the crisis at hand, justify and explain their actions, and continue to retain control over the situation. This is a difficult task, particularly in view of the fact that they are under constant scrutiny from the government, political representatives of the people, the public as well as other interested groups in society.

Another dimension of the issue deserves attention. In providing public services, attention is focused on those areas that have traditionally been considered as core functions of the government. Hood and Schupert suggested that "defining", or principal functions of the government, such as the maintenance of law and order and the collection of revenue, were performed by "core" government enterprise, while the physical resource mobilisation functions, i.e. activities related to infrastructure such as transport, were most salient to independent public enterprises (1988, p. 8). Studies on the performance of public management thus focus on the tasks and activities that contribute to concrete output, such as the construction and operation of facilities, and the implementation of health and education programmes. It is possible to provide an account of such activities, and demonstrate results by the number of facilities constructed, the rate of usage by the public, a decreasing number of patients seeking medical care, and an increasing number of skilled and employable graduates.

In recent years, there has been an increased emphasis on the appraisal of public officials, and performance is measured on the basis of a number of indicators. Although there is widespread disagreement on the construction, use and reliability of indicators for performance in the public sector, the tendency has been to measure performance with reference to those activities whose results can be quantified, and "what gets measured gets done" (Likierman, 1993). Therefore, Flynn suggests, "If performance measurement is to improve performance, all the relevant measures must be made, not just those that are easy to count" (1997, p. 185).

This is the neglected area that needs closer attention. Public managers get engrossed in performing tasks that yield concrete output, and are prone to ignore other sets of activities that are of equal, if not more, importance. These tasks involve instilling and inculcating public confidence in the administrative system. The community develops a positive sense of good public management, with the impression that the system is being operated on the basis of fair rules. The public managers are viewed as efficient and effective, with the understanding that the system is transparent with an open channel of communication between the government and the public. It is necessary to create a sense of security based on the rule of law, which ensures equal and fair treatment to all. At the same time, it is essential to present an informed and competent image to the public. These activities, which do not produce tangible output, constitute an important element of public management. It appears that a lack of attention to such areas of intangible public service, contributed to a considerable extent to the escalation of apparently minor problems into crises in Hong Kong.

Nature of Crises in Hong Kong

Any situation which calls for a deviation from existing arrangements may be described as a crisis. Public sector managers in Hong Kong have faced a number of situations in the years since the handover to China. Let us examine the nature of crises faced by Hong Kong and determine the location of the problem. The cases depicted in this study indicate an extensive area of coverage. While some of the events could be viewed as minor deviations from the established practice under changing circumstances, others placed the public managers at considerable risk. Often, minor deviations erupted into full-fledged crises due to the style of management adopted by public managers.

Crises can be deceptive in appearance and substance. Apparently innocuous conditions can be followed by drastic changes, and this can affect the ability of a public official to identify the precipitation of a crisis and act on it. The five steps suggested by Rosenthal and Kouzmin (1997) involve raising questions about prevailing social, economic and technological priorities, and the dilemma of restoration as opposed to adaptation or innovation.

Among the cases under review, the resignation of the Director of Immigration was not viewed as a matter that could give rise to public concern. The government viewed it as a personnel decision, which was handled in accordance with existing rules. It could have been perceived that way, had the case not been made prominent by subsequent developments. Senior officials did not take into consideration the social and political context under which the decision was made. First, residents of Hong Kong were suffering from a high level of anxiety due to the impending reversal of sovereignty to China. Every move by the government was being carefully watched, and the sudden resignation of the chief of a critical government agency was bound to attract questions.

Moreover, speculation was rife about the loss of expertise and experience due to massive emigration throughout the first half of the 1990s. But the government did not seem to be aware of the level of anxiety in society as a result of the departure of capable public managers. The resignation of Leung, the Director of Immigration, shortly before 1997 needed careful consideration, and completely transparent procedure had to be maintained.

The case also brought to the fore a significant development in Hong Kong's political system. The Legislative Council was being democratised in phases and it was composed of directly-elected members by 1995. For the first time, Hong Kong had a group of legislators who were answerable to the electorate. This group had to carve out their territory in the extremely protected territory of Hong Kong policy and administration, and in asserting their position, was soon confronted by a hostile bureaucracy. The government was mistaken in assuming that they could intimidate the legislators into submission and the endorsement of policies proposed by senior public officials. This strategy also turned out to be counterproductive and the Leung case attained more significance in this aspect. The conflict between the executive and the legislature indicated a rift, which will perhaps have an influence on Hong Kong politics for a long time.

Eventually, the Leung case took the form of a debate regarding two issues. First, the government tried to establish the fact that major decisions can be made in the public interest, and the government should be allowed to suppress the assumptions behind such decisions. Using the pretext of public argument, the government sought to retain the right not to disclose details of cases such as Leung's. The public, media and members of the Legislative Council found it difficult to accept that the government could operate under a cloak of secrecy, using public interest as an excuse. The debate centred on the issue of what the government should and should not be allowed to conceal in an era of democratic and transparent governance in Hong Kong.

Secondly, Hong Kong was navigating uncharted waters in the sense that the relationship between the traditionally dominant executive and a fully-elected legislature had not been firmly established. The case came as a test of the strength of democratic institutions in Hong Kong. To their credit, members of the Legislative Council were able to stake their ground in this battle, and the media contributed its share to the establishment of a transparent form of administration. Unfortunately, the political reforms, which had helped to establish effective political control over the bureaucracy, were terminated with the scrapping of the elected legislature with effect from 1 July 1997.

The "bird flu" case was an entirely different type of crisis. The major challenge, in the initial stages, appeared to be understanding and providing a clear explanation of the origin of the virus that struck Hong Kong. In the early stages, public managers sought to treat the crisis as another minor problem in the routine task of ensuring safety and hygiene in the poultry markets. They appeared to be willing the problem away, and were perceived to be quite confident that the issue was an isolated death and there was no need to address the public's concerns or alleviate their fears. Armed with limited information, public managers sought to assure the public that the problem had been successfully resolved. Apparently, this was a case related to the management of public health, although the crisis escalated due to the lack, and sometimes poor handling of information by public officials.

However, a careful analysis indicates that a number of factors were clouding the major issues to be tackled. While the steps to determine the origin and communication of the virus were essential, the public managers seemed to neglect the important task of keeping the public informed about the progress of investigation and its implications for society. With such a health scare looming, particularly as it was linked to a very popular element of the public's diet, chicken, the government demonstrated a lack of initiative that reflected poorly on its capability to manage crises. While the public was extremely nervous about consuming chicken, they were treated to frivolous and irresponsible statements by senior public officials. Such an approach to the management of the crisis only added to the confusion that existed at the time. Moreover, in assessing the situation and arriving at a decision, the interests of the various stakeholders did not appear to receive adequate attention. It should be admitted that the government did not possess all the information at the outset, but this fact was not communicated to the public in a reassuring manner.

The lack of an adequate system of information dissemination affected the management of the crisis. However, it was exacerbated by the bizarre decision to slaughter every chicken in Hong Kong. It has not been possible to examine the process through which this decision was reached, but it may be safe to suggest that the government had the good intention of eliminating the problem once and for all by killing all the chickens, whether they had the virus, or not. This decision appeared as a sudden and somewhat impractical solution to a problem that could have had serious consequences for the health of consumers of chicken, the livelihood of stakeholders in the poultry industry, the operation itself, and the perception of the public of the competence of public managers.

The chaos and confusion witnessed during the culling confirmed the perception of incompetence of public officials. It had an adverse impact on the morale of the officials, and revealed the flaws in the solution chosen by the government to manage the crisis. As the time scheduled by the government was found to be inadequate, it further led credence to the view that the crisis was not competently managed. Problems could be found in the manner of co-ordination employed between the employees of the Health Department and those of the Agriculture and Fisheries Department who were entrusted with the task of implementing the decision to cull chickens. A lack of understanding, preparation, and ability to carry out the task as planned indicated the government's failure to manage the crisis. In addition, the absence of the Chief Executive and other senior public officials at the earlier stages of the crisis affected the public's confidence. Subsequently, with the installation of the Chief Secretary for Administration as the head of the team managing the crisis, public confidence was somewhat restored. Yet it could not return to the high level of confidence previously enjoyed by the Hong Kong public service.

The case relating to the circulation of the *Hong Kong Standard* newspaper and the prosecution of some individuals, acquired great significance for Hong Kong, particularly in view of the fact that it took place shortly after the reversal of sovereignty to the People's Republic of China. The continuation of the rule of law in Hong Kong has been a major source of concern ever since the signing of the Joint Declaration between Great Britain and China in 1984. It was a legitimate concern, since the legal systems followed in Hong Kong and China are quite different. Moreover, it was felt that legal procedures could be influenced by political and other external considerations, and the course of justice could be affected in cases adjudicated in Hong Kong after 1997.

The case relating to the non-prosecution of Sally Aw was perceived as a test of public confidence in the continuation of the rule of law in Hong Kong. The rule of law ensures that everyone is treated equally in the eyes of the justice system, and there should be no deviation for any reason. Hence, the decision by the Secretary for Justice not to prosecute one of the four persons listed as alleged conspirators on the charge sheet, while proceeding with the prosecution of the other three, could be viewed as a breach of the rule of law. Grave apprehension was expressed over the perceived lack of neutrality in the judicial system. In this case, there was no scope for misunderstanding the extent of the crisis.

The Basic Law of the Hong Kong Special Administrative region of the People's Republic of China states:

> The laws previously in force in Hong Kong, that is, the common law, rules of equity, ordinances, subordinate legislation and customary law shall be maintained, except for any that contravene this Law, and subject to any amendment by the legislature of the Hong Kong Special Administrative Region" (Article 8), and that "All Hong Kong residents shall be equal before the law" (Article 25).

Accordingly, much of the anxiety regarding the continuation of rule of law was alleviated in the run up to the handover.

The case of Sally Aw was tempered by a number of events that highlighted weaknesses in the judicial independence of the Secretary for Justice. The non-prosecution of the Xinhua News Agency (an official agency of the Chinese Foreign Office) for breaching the *Personal Data (Privacy) Ordinance* in 1996 had given rise to concern over the limited authority exercised by the Secretary for Justice. Other developments around that time seemed to support the general view that decisions of the Justice

Department were considerably influenced by political and other external factors. However, the failure to convince the community that the rule of law was being upheld constituted the core of the crisis.

As events progressed, the focus appeared to be shifting towards the role of the Secretary for Justice. Her lack of appropriate experience in the legal business and the political basis of her appointment were brought up as possible reasons for her inability to contain the crisis. She rejected all speculation that her decision was based on political considerations or was made under pressure from the government, but was not convincing in providing justifications for her decision.

The explanations provided by the Secretary of Justice and the vague statements made by the Chief Executive on the issue, yet again underlined the weakness of the Hong Kong government in managing information. Other than repeating that the rule of law was effective in Hong Kong, the Chief Executive had practically nothing to say. The Secretary for Justice, on her part, made lengthy statements without offering explanations for the decision. The lack of organised and credible information escalated the level of anxiety and the crisis erupted as a major source of embarrassment for the government. Presenting the facts to the public and the legislators was an issue, but the basic problem was much more serious.

Few steps were taken to inform the public, rationalise the decision, and deal with the crisis. It is most likely that there was no scope for rationalising such a decision. The eventual conviction of three out of the four conspirators suggests that Sally Aw has been given special treatment by the government. The case also raises the issue of the capability of senior public managers, as the Secretary for Justice appeared to be out of her depth in managing the crisis. Although the government worked hard at controlling the damage at the late stages, public confidence in the rule of law and the capability of the Secretary of Justice could not be fully restored.

The case of Hong Kong International Airport is quite different in nature from the other cases in this collection. Although there are implications for the management of public services, the problems encountered in inaugurating the airport could be viewed as mainly related to organisational matters. The crisis was obviously precipitated by the sudden decision to bring forward the opening date of the airport. There could be many reasons behind that decision, but a popular explanation has been the visits at that time of the Presidents of the People's Republic of China and the United States of America to Hong Kong. Many observers believe that the date was shifted to coincide with the visit of these dignitaries, and overlooked various other considerations that should have formed the basis of such a decision. It is not desirable to allow political considerations to influence such matters, particularly regarding facilities which involved the safety of numerous air travellers.

As the case progressed, several other issues emerged. There was confusion as to the leadership of the project and its failure to prevent this outcome in such a prestigious project. On one level, the design and construction of the airport was managed by a group of specialists who were competent in technical aspects and could make decisions of an operational nature. At another level, this group of specialists was supervised by a number of generalists composed of senior civil servants, members of the legislature and other prominent public personalities.

As the airport was being constructed, many of the problems associated with the allocation of responsibilities did not surface. While the specialists were allowed autonomy to function without interference from the generalists, the operation appeared to be progressing smoothly. Periodic overviews by the generalists were considered to be a good system of monitoring the work. Tension between specialists and generalists was not obvious at this stage, and the problem of striking a balance between delegation and centralisation did not emerge.

But the relationships and dynamics changed with the eruption of the crisis on the day the airport was opened for operation. As a number of systems malfunctioned, both the public and the media were curious about the reasons. As the world's largest infrastructure project at the time, this was considered to be an unacceptable case of mismanagement. The huge outcry over the problems triggered a number of investigations into the causes, and the search was on for identifying the reasons for the crisis. Subsequent reports seemed to place the major share of the blame on the specialists, who were engaged in the design and construction of the airport.

Interestingly, the major turning point for the crisis could be pinpointed to the date for opening the airport. Apparently, work was going on well and the different components of the project were at various points of readiness, when suddenly it was decided to open the airport in early July. This may have caught the specialists by surprise, and the results reflect problems in the decision-making process. The origin of the crisis can thus be linked to the adoption of an arbitrary decision, made without consulting the managers who would be responsible for delivering the results. As the decision to determine an opening date was influenced by political considerations, the government and its leaders were not inclined to seek the opinions of the specialists.

The manner in which the decision was reached revealed another aspect of crisis in public management. Channels of communication were closed and ineffective between the specialists and generalists and there were divisions and disagreements even within these two groups. As a consequence, the government could not be informed of the potential problems in advancing the opening date of such a huge project. On the other hand, the specialists were apparently not fully aware of the determination of the government to open the airport on a particular day. The full implications of such a decision were unknown to either group. Eventually, the process of groupthink may have set in, and all concerned groups were convinced in their subconscious mind that it would be possible to open the airport early.

In reviewing the aftermath caused by the airport opening prior to the scheduled date, problems with the planning process cannot be overlooked. In any group activity, all sections must be consulted and a consensus reached over the feasibility of a proposed decision. This did not happen in the case of the airport. By the same token, the problem of co-ordination was worsened, due to a poor system of monitoring progress and holding managers accountable. Although a supervisory body had been appointed, this group was unable to exert much influence due to their lack of specialist knowledge. However, when the decision to open the airport was made, the views of the specialists were not taken into consideration. This also led to the escalation of conflict among personalities. This became clear after a number of major problems were encountered after the airport was opened. The effort to place blame on each other by the two groups supports this view.

In retrospect, the four cases point to problems in various aspects of the management of public services. The major issues are related to the definition and protection of public interest, the organisation and dissemination of accurate and adequate information at times of crises, the continuation and protection of rule of law, and the establishment of a decision-making system in which public managers have an opportunity to participate along with the political executive.

Areas of Concentration and Neglect

A particular pattern of behaviour can be discerned among public managers in Hong Kong in dealing with crises, and a number of points can be highlighted from the cases under review. This can help to identify the causes of the crises, and develop strategies to minimise the impact of their consequences. These relate to the ability and competence of public managers, the nature of relationships in the system, and the facilities required for managing crises.

All the cases reflect a consistent inability to anticipate the onset of a crisis. Except for the bird flu case, the other crises emerged from apparently innocuous situations. The sudden resignation of a senior public servant and the non-prosecution of an influential personality are critical events, but such deviation from established procedures could have been dealt with in a more efficient manner. The government and its officials could have been prevented the events from blowing up into full-fledged crises through careful monitoring. The government should have been able to read the mood of the community under the highly-charged and tense circumstances preceding and following the reversal of sovereignty to China. Sensitive areas of operation such as immigration and judicial matters were susceptible to the prospects of misunderstandings and adversely affecting public opinion. Public managers should have been able to anticipate the consequences of sensitive decisions and prepare themselves for the community's reaction before such actions were taken.

Hong Kong has benefited from the service of capable and experienced civil servants and this has, naturally, heightened the expectations of the public. It is quite likely that there were public managers who were aware of the developments taking place in these cases. However, the tradition of colonial public administration was faithfully followed, and there was no attempt to draw the attention of the relevant department and the government to the impending crises. Alerting colleagues and appropriate authorities about potential problems is considered a part of effective management in the public sector.

A third area of concern is the lack of ability to compile and comprehend information relevant to the crises confronted by the public managers. It is understandable that in some cases such as the bird flu incident, it took some time to acquire accurate and detailed information on the virus. Yet the agencies concerned demonstrated their inability to compile and assimilate the relevant information before preparing reports that could be presented to the public and the media. Although the crisis of the airport's opening remained the focus of public attention for a long period of time, there appeared to be contradictory and often inadequate information in the hands of public managers.

Related issues seemed to be the lack of facilities and ability to disseminate the information that was collected. At various stages of the crisis, one of the senior public managers made statements which did not help in explaining implications or point towards solutions. The situation worsened with the incoherent and vague statements made by the Chief Executive. Obviously, a lack of communication between the public and the government was found to be a major problem in all the crises. With a better system of informing the public and reassuring them, much of the anxiety could be reduced and damage to the reputation of the government could be contained.

Under Hong Kong's new political arrangements, the relationship between the executive and legislature emerges as a critical element in the management of crises in the public sector. Political reforms did not have a smooth introduction in Hong Kong, and the traditional style of government is still being practised. Consequently, Hong Kong's revered executive-led style continues, oblivious to the new realities. Little importance is attached to the sentiments of the public or their representatives, and the powerful executive rules Hong Kong through arbitrary decisions, strong statements and entertains no questions. Therefore, in most of the cases, there was little interest or scope for participation by stakeholders other than public managers, in planning and implementing measures to manage the crises.

Co-ordination of the various sections of a department and the agencies of government is extremely important in managing crises. In the case of natural disasters, "a large number of public agencies are brought together to deal with emergencies and provide a vast number of services ranging from maintenance of order and security (restrictive role) to search and rescue missions (proactive role) to provision of shelter, comfort and rehabilitation (compassionate/encouraging role)" (Huque, 1998, p. 105). Similarly, crisis situations in the management of public services require a number of responses simultaneously, and often these are provided by diverse public agencies. Unless the activities of such agencies are planned and co-ordinated in an effective manner, all effort will be futile. In the cases analysed in this study, there were numerous indications of poor co-ordination among public agencies. The government and the Legislative Council were at odds on many occasions and appeared to be working against one another rather than in the desired mode of co-ordination. Hence overlapping and contradictions in the roles and positions of the government and its various departments (Immigration, Health, Agriculture and Fisheries, Judiciary, and Transport) appeared to be ill co-ordinated and contributed to its image as a monolithic and incompetent bureaucracy.

The adversarial relationship between the government and the legislature is further reflected in the decision of an active and popular member of the Legislative Council, Christine Loh, not to seek re-election to the council in the next round of elections. She alleged "The executive branch's fear of sharing power is stunting the development of the political system", and added that the Executive Council "sees the legislature as an inconvenience that has to be overcome rather than as an active partner to build participatory governance" (*South China Morning Post*, 12th April 2000). A harmonious relationship between these two critical institutions could have been extremely useful in managing the crises. Instead of focusing on the non-performance and weaknesses of each other, the representatives of the people and the executive could have worked together toward the resolution of problems.

Finally, the cases reveal that an important area of public management has been neglected in Hong Kong. It appears that the government was relying on the past success of the public services and did not pay adequate attention to the retention and improvement of its image. In modern societies, it is not enough for governments to perform their job while maintaining a distance from the community. There must be arrangements and facilities for engaging in constant communication. Persistent effort must be made at keeping the public informed about the achievements of the government and explaining measures adopted in managing various aspects of public services. In particular, difficulties faced in dealing with certain issues must be explained to the stakeholders and any other group interested in the process. The packaging of such information has emerged as an essential skill in modern governments. Hong Kong was slow to catch on to the trend and suffered by way of miscommunication and misunderstanding in the management of crises. Although belatedly, an information co-ordinator has been appointed by the Hong Kong government, and this office was subsequently seen to be active in co-ordinating information and communicating with the public and the media.

Lessons to be Learned

How can crises in the provision of public services be effectively managed? The answer is related to the enhancement of quality of management in the public sector, and a wide range of studies is available for providing guidance. Peters and Waterman (1982) based their study on organisations in the private sector in the United States of America and found that their success was due to a bias for action, keeping close contact with customers, developing productivity through people, staying hands-on and value driven, and allowing autonomy and entrepreneurship. Denhardt reviewed several studies and found that a number of elements were identified in contributing to the success of organisations. These include delegation of authority and responsibility, shared decision-making, participation and involvement, trust and integrity, emphasis on people, participative leadership, innovative work styles, a strong client orientation, and a mindset that seeks optimum performance (Denhardt, 1992, pp. 4-5).

Most of these values are not to be found in the traditional bureaucratic set up. Such ideas have been ushered in with the introduction of "new public administration" (for details see the volume edited by Marini, 1971), and later in the same decade subsequently elaborated and firmly established in the formulation of "new public management". The public services in Hong Kong have been managed under a traditional framework for a long period of time and hence even minor deviations and temporary lapses gave rise to situations which easily assumed crises proportions. Apparently, simple issues were complicated by the political and social environment immediately before and after the reversal of sovereignty to China.

It should also be borne in mind that traditional bureaucratic values play a useful role in the performance of management functions in the public sector. The pyramidal structure of administrative organisations is still found to be the most appropriate for large-scale operations in the public sector. The concepts of division of labour, co-ordination, scalar and functional processes, span of control, and unity of command still influence the organisation of administrative activities. Gulick and Urwick (1937) highlighted seven of types of activities - planning, organising, staffing, directing, co-ordinating, reporting, and budgeting (POSDCORB) - that constitute the principal functions of administration.

Obviously, while these seven activities form the basis of operating administrative organisations in routine functions, values such as delegation, participatory decision-making, client orientation and innovation are of great importance in managing crises in the public sector. Problems are encountered as many organisations place more emphasis on the POSDCORB. This is with the objective of ensuring regularity and objectivity, and has the advantage of standardising procedures and practices. Such an arrangement does not allow adequate facilities for new values to develop and this, in turn, affects the ability of public managers to perform to the best of their ability during a crisis. This defensive position of public organisations has been responsible for several criticisms that have been levelled at them in recent years.

The experience of Hong Kong suggests that a mixture of both types of values, with each accorded equal importance, should be used in the design and operation of public organisations. By transmitting the message that upholding standardised procedures will help maintain the current level of service, while innovation and a participatory approach will lead to improvements, governments can promote new values and seek to incorporate better patterns of behaviour among public managers. They will be aware of the fact that deviating from established patterns of behaviour may even be rewarded, and that will prepare them better to perform in the event of challenges that are non-routine in nature.

It is time to alert public managers to the importance of the intangible output of public organisations. It is no longer adequate to concentrate on the simple production and delivery of public services. Along with the routine tasks, public managers must become proficient in dealing with non-routine situations. As a preparatory measure to deal with unforeseen contingencies, there should be a constant effort to present the organisation and operation of public entities in a positive light. At the same time, there should be a proactive role in promoting and protecting the public's confidence in the system. This can be achieved by dealing with crises confidently, efficiently and according to established rules and regulations.

Public managers must be equipped with adequate information in dealing with crises as well as regular administrative matters. According to Zinke, "those who work and live in public organizations are conceived as technological artifacts - information processors - who can be spiritually manipulated and environmentally conditioned to instrumentally achieve the goals and visions of the communal artificers" (1990, p. 198). In most cases in this study, problems were exacerbated due to a lack of adequate and relevant information. It is also important to disseminate the available information to all public managers involved in the process of dealing with a crisis.

Of equal importance to the issue of keeping the community informed of the nature and extent of crises, are their likely impact and steps to be taken for containing the damage. If the government is overwhelmed by a crisis and concentrates on managing it without communicating with the community, rumours and speculations may cause substantial damage to the effort of public managers. Communication and consultation with the public must be conducted in an organised and coherent manner, and should not contradict the views of the major protagonists. Special care should be taken to present an efficient and competent front, while ensuring that the messages reflect the reality.

The political executive must undertake its responsibility for managing crises. This task should not be left to the public sector managers alone. The adversarial relationship witnessed between the executive and the legislature during the emergence of crises in Hong Kong underlines the need for forging an effective executive-legislative partnership. The executive must not view the efforts of the legislature as excuses to find faults, and identify organisations and individuals in the public sector for blame. On their part, members of the legislature need to approach their task as partners of the executive in governance, and exercise utmost discretion in performing their role. The development of a culture of partnership between the executive and legislature could go a long way in preparing governments to manage crises in the public sector.

As governments govern for the sake of public interest, care should be taken to ensure that it is not compromised. The definition of "public interest" will remain a major challenge, as political and other interest groups will seek to promote their own points of view in this area. Some of the complications could be eliminated by opening up the system of public management and emphasising maximum transparency in public affairs. The free flow of information and a clear indication of the costs and benefits of major public decisions could facilitate such an approach. It will be a significant step forward if these elements are incorporated into the culture of public management, along with concrete incentives for recognising contributions in these areas by public officials.

In addition to the lessons mentioned above, the basic values of public management practised over the years must also be maintained. The structure, lines of authority, channels of communication, methods of co-ordination, and other such elements will ensure the smooth operation of public organisations. Innovation and continuous effort at improvement will have to become part of the process to allow public organisations to perform at the highest level of efficiency. At times of crises in particular, the management of public services will have to transcend narrow organisational and institutional boundaries and jurisdictions, to allow public managers maximum facilities for dealing with crises in their organisations.

Governments employ a variety of measures, structures and strategies in order to secure optimum results in the provision of public services. It is necessary to understand these elements in greater depth to obtain insights and ideas which can be useful in prescribing ways and means for managing public services. Occasionally, public officials are unable to resolve a problem and the government is confronted with a crisis. This study examined a number of attempts by the government and public officials to manage crises. In the process, the causes of the crises, methods employed to deal with them, and their impact have been highlighted. The crises provided an opportunity to learn from failure and this will be useful in drawing lessons as it opens a window on the dynamics, organisation and management of government. Crises in the management of public services are an undesirable but inevitable aspect of government. The best strategy to manage crisis is to remain alert and perform the required duties, bearing in mind the intangible along with the tangible aspects of public management.

Appendix 1

Crisis: Retirement of a Senior Civil Servant

1965	Leung joins the Civil Service
1989	Appointed Director of Immigration
1993	Leung's 22 year old daughter, Sylvia Leung Sze-hon is murdered in the carpark of the British Columbia Institute of Technology in Canada
October 1995	ICAC raids Leung's home and office
November 1995	Commencement of routine extended integrity checks by the police outside of ICAC investigation
April 1996	ICAC sends a letter of apology to Leung confirming that allegations against him were unsubstantiated
May 1996	Chief Secretary (CS) receives report on Leung submitted to the ICAC's Operations Review Committee (ORC report)
June 1996	Civil Service Bureau receives Leung's failed integrity check report
4 July 1996	Secretary of Civil Service (SCS), Lam Woon-kwong invites Leung to a meeting on July 5
5 July 1996	10 a.m.: Leung meets with SCS
	4:00 p.m.: Leung submits retirement notice and a request for waiver of the regular period of notice

5:25 p.m.:   SCS sends approval letter to Leung confirming waiver of the period of notice and stating retirement would have immediate effect

SCS notifies Acting Chief Secretary (Donald Tsang) and the Secretary for Security by phone

Evening: SCS invites Director-General of Industry Regina Ip Lau Suk-yee to a meeting the following morning

Leung meets Chen Zuo'er, China's representative in the Sino-British Join Liaison Group (JLG), at a coffee shop in Wan Chai for a ten minute chat and tells Mr. Chen that he is going to retire

6 July 1996   9:30 a.m.: Xinhua informed of Leung's retirement

Morning: SCS offers Regina Ip the job and she accepts

Noon: Announcement of Leung's retirement

Governor Patten leaves for trip to Europe

8 July 1996   Deputy to the Governor, Donald Tsang comments: "We respect his [Leung's] personal wish. We won't make public the reason for his retirement."

9 July 1996   Leung makes public comments on his retirement outside his Shouson Hill Home

Governor Chris Patten comments on the same from Europe

Joint Liaison Group representative Chen Zuo'er also comments

10 July 1996   Director of the Hong Kong and Macau Affairs Office, Lu Ping comments on Leung's case

	SCS emphasises confidentiality of retirement matters
11 July 1996	SCS attends Special Public Service Panel Meeting
15 July 1996	Governor Patten returns to Hong Kong after his European tour
16 July 1996	Donald Tsang Yam-kuen comments on the government's duty to protect the privacy of civil servants
	Official announcement of Director-General of Industry Regina Ip Lau Suk-yee's appointment as the first woman immigration chief
August 1996	Public Service Panel agrees to hold an inquiry into the sudden retirement of the immigration chief
September 1996	Special House Committee meets to consider the Report of the Panel on Public Service on the inquiry into the circumstances surrounding the retirement of Leung, former Director of Immigration
4 October 1996	House Committee endorses wording for the proposed motion recommended by subcommittee
23 October 1996	Legislative Council Motion debate on the appointment of Select Committee
25 October 1996	House Committee agrees to recommend to the President 10 members to the Select Committee
1 November 1996	House Committee members agree to recommend to the President the appointment of Dr Philip Wong Yu-hong as a member, raising the total membership to 11
8 November 1996	Morning: Select Committee decides that all witnesses would be required to take an oath or

make an affirmation before giving evidence

Afternoon: House Committee considers the Report of the Select Committee on procedures in regard to determination of claims of "public interest immunity"

15 November 1996   House Committee decides on further business for the Legco sitting on 20 November 1996

20 November 1996   Legco Motion Debate

22 November 1996   SCS testifies at the second meeting of the Select Committee, and produces the application for retirement submitted by Leung along with the approval letter issued the same day

5 December 1996   SCS's personal assistant Eda Chan, Deputy Director of Immigration, and the new Director of Immigration, Regina Ip testify at the third meeting of the Select Committee

12 December 1996   Deputy Secretary for the Civil Service Sandra Lee Suk-yee, Secretary for Security, Peter Lai Hing-ling, and the Financial Secretary testify at the fourth meeting of the Select Committee

10 January 1997   Leung testifies at the fifth meeting of the Select Committee

An anonymous caller on a RTHK [Radio Television Hong Kong] phone-in program reveals seeing Leung meet Chen Zuo'er, a Chinese representative in the Sino-British Joint Liaison Group, in the afternoon of July 5

Government responds to Leung's statement

11 January 1997   Government continues to defend its position in the case

15 January 1997   SCS testifies for the second time at the sixth

meeting of the Select Committee revealing details of the meeting with Leung on 5 July

Leung refutes the government's testimony on rumours over his retirement

16 January 1997 Media publish reports on Leung's business partners

Select Committee demands the disclosure of the integrity report and the ICAC's Operations Review Committee Report on Leung

17 January 1997 Governor Patten meets with policy secretaries to discuss the demand of the Select Committee to release ICAC and integrity check reports on Leung

22 January 1997 Select Committee receives evidence (letter from the commissioner of the ICAC, an edited 3 hour interview with Mr Leung and an edited summary of the Police's integrity check report) from CS at the seventh meeting of the Select Committee

28 January 1997 Secretary for Security testifies to the Select Committee for the second time

29 January 1997 SCS answers questions at a Select Committee meeting

21 February 1997 Tenth Select Committee meeting

Deputy Commissioner of Police summoned to explain to legislators extended integrity checks in a closed door session

28 February 1997 Leung testifies at the eleventh meeting of the Select Committee and members request his permission for public disclosure of the edited ICAC interview tapes

11 March 1997	Select Committee writes to the CS stating the view that [the Committee] should not be deprived of any substantive material upon which the Government had relied to reach the decision to initiate CR (Colonial regulation) 59 action against Leung
12 April 1997	Civil Service Bureau informs the Select Committee that the CS, after further consultation with the Commissioner of ICAC and legal advisers, remained of the view that it would not be in the public interest to disclose the ORC Report to the Committee
17 April 1997	Summons issued to CS advising her to produce the ORC Report to the Committee on 24 April 1997
21 April 1997	CS issues a "Certificate of Chief Secretary" to the Select Committee stating again that production of the ORC report is injurious to the public interest and that the disclosure of the Report is not necessary to enable the Committee to fairly examine the circumstances of Leung's departure or any directly related matter
22 April 1997	Legal Department applies for a judicial declaration of immunity allowing CS not to disclose the ICAC report on Leung
24 April 1997	CS refuses to produce the ORC report on the ground of public interest immunity and, according to the procedures of the Legislative Council Resolution, explains the reasons to the Chairman in confidence
9 May 1997	Chairman states that CS had not provided sufficient justification for not producing a copy of the ORC report for the sake of public interest Select Committee orders CS to produce an edited version of the original ORC report

15 May 1997	CS produces an edited version of the ORC report to Chairman of Select Committee
19 May 1997	Select Committee Chairman Ip Kwok-him issues a statement on the Operations Review Committee report (ICAC Report) on Leung
	Select Committee withdraws demand for full disclosure of the ICAC ORC Report
	Legal proceedings discontinued by Attorney General
11 June 1997	Report of the Select Committee to Inquire into the circumstances surrounding the Departure of Mr Leung Ming-yin from the Government and related issues released
18 June 1997	Legislative Council Motion debate to endorse the Report of the Select Committee
2 December 1997	Leung tries to gain support from the NPC [National People's Committee] selection panel members

Appendix 2

Crisis: Bird Flu

May 1997	First Victim of Bird Flu, a three-year-old boy, dies at Queen Elizabeth Hospital in Hong Kong
June 1997	Samples forwarded to the Center for Disease Control (CDC) in the United States, Mill Hill in the United Kingdom, and the National Institute of Health and the Environment in the Netherlands
10 August 1997	H5N1 virus identified as the cause of the child's death
18 August 1997	CDC sends written confirmation that the virus was H5N1
20 August 1997	Department of Health of Hong Kong Government announces the world's first case of H5N1 infection in humans
21 August 1997	Taskforce to deal with the problem found
8 September 1997	The Health Services Panel of the Provisional Legislative Council meets
9 November 1997	Second victim of Bird Flu survives as a two-year old boy makes a full recovery and is discharged from hospital
28 November 1997	Director of Health reveals details about the second victim in a press conference

5 December 1997	Bird Flu wipes out a third of chickens at a stall in a Fan Ling public housing estate
6 December 1997	Director of Health reveals information on two more victims of Bird Flu: a 54-year-old man and a 13-year-old girl
9 December 1997	Health Services Panel of the Provisional Legislative Council meets
10 December 1997	Government issues guidelines to schools and kindergartens on the prevention of bird flu
11 December 1997	Director of Health tells citizens not to be afraid of eating chicken and adds that she herself ate chicken daily.
12 December 1997	Doctors request for more information on the virus, illness and treatment
16 December 1997	Director of Health announces the possibility of human-to-human transmission of H5N1
20 December 1997	Chicken farmers demand action against the problem
24 December 1997	China orders a temporary ban on chicken exported to Hong Kong
29 December 1997	Government decides to slaughter all local poultry, estimated at approximately 1.2 million in a 24-hour operation, and the operationwhich reveals various aspects of poor planning, inefficiency and lack of effectiveness
31 December 1997	Health Services Panel of the Provisional Legislative Council meets
2 January 1998	Government admits slaughter was not conducted smoothly

7 January 1998	Government agrees to increase compensation to chicken farmers
11 January 1998	Director of Health claims slaughter to be effective since no new cases of bird flu had been detected
14 January 1998	A group of thirteen delegates from the World Health Organization (WHO) enters China on a surveillance mission
16 January 1998	WHO rules out China as source of H5N1 and points to dirty chicken farms and markets in Hong Kong
18 January 1998	WHO warns that another six-month period of careful surveillance would be necessary before determining if the H5N1 virus has had been reasonably contained in Hong Kong
20 January 1998	Delegates of the WHO group clears chicken from China and says Hong Kong could lift ban when ready
6 February 1998	Ban on import of chickens lifted
7 February 1998	38,000 chickens from the first batch after lifting of the ban arrive in Hong Kong from China
24 February 1998	Ban lifted on five local chicken farms for the first time since the slaughter
21 April 1998	Findings at the First International Symposium on Adult Immunization in Asia reveal that one in five chickens in Hong Kong's markets carried the bird flu, suggesting that Hong Kong the territory may have prevented an epidemic by the slaughter and segregation of chickens from other fowl
1 May 1998	New import controls set up for the importation of ducks

28 January 1999   Director of Health, Dr. Margaret Chan and Professor Ken Shortridge of the Department of Microbiology at the University of Hong Kong receive Thailand's Prince Mahildol Award for their contribution towards public health measures for successfully averting the bird flu outbreak

Appendix 3

**Crisis: Non-Prosecution of a Prominent Personality and Xinhua News
Agency, and the Right of Abode Controversy**

July 1997

Provisional Legislative Council rushes through
laws requiring children [whose parents became
permanent residents of Hong Kong after their birth
or were born in China] to obtain Certificates of
Entitlement from outside Hong Kong before
immigration

February 1998

Xinhua News Agency not prosecuted for
contravening the *Personal Data (Privacy)
Ordinance 1996*

March 1998

Chief Executive says that the Xinhua case was one
of "technical violation, not a substantive breach"

ICAC investigations reveal a conspiracy by
between the Chairman of the

Sing Tao Group Sally Aw Sian with and three
executives of the daily newspaper the *Hong Kong
Standard* to "defraud purchasers of advertising
space ... by various dishonest means"

The three executives are charged with conspiring
to inflate the paper's circulation figure

Chairman of the Group Sally Aw is not prosecuted

Department of Justice issues a press statement on
the policy of prosecution to defend its position

	Martin Lee reminds the community that no individual or organisation is above the rule of law
April 1998	Secretary for Justice invited to give account at a special meeting for the Provisional Legislative Council's Panel on Administration of Justice and Legal Services
	Provisional Legislative Council amends the *Adaptation to Laws (Interpretive Provisions) Bill*, exempting authorities and their subordinate agencies from some local laws [including the *Privacy Ordinance*] retrospective to 1 July 1997
May 1998	Government lodges appeal against January 1998 decision of Court of First Instance that mainland-born offspring of Hong Kong residents automatically acquire right of abode in the territory
	Court of Final Appeal overrules Court of First Instance on the right of abode case
January 1999	Trial of three executives of the *Hong Kong Standard* concludes and they are convicted
February 1999	Court of Final Appeal rules that immigration laws cannot be made retrospective and gives Hong Kong courts the power to interfere in the decisions of the National People's Congress (NPC) of the People's Republic of China if they it contravenes the *Basic Law*
	In a long statement to the Legislative Council's Panel on Administration of Justice and Legal Services, Secretary for Justice explains the reasons for non-prosecution of Aw as "insufficient evidence" and "public interest"
	Legislators raise questions about the Secretary of Justice's definition of "public interest"
	Survey shows a 31% drop in the level of

confidence in the administration of justice in Hong Kong, an apparent effect of the statement of the Secretary for Justice

Secretary for Justice meets legal experts from China to discuss the constitutional crisis

Secretary for Justice announces that the central government [of China] believed that part of the Court of Final Appeal's judgement on the right of abode breached the constitution, and the *Basic Law* required amendment

March 1999

Legislator Margaret Ng unsuccessfully moves a motion on a vote of no confidence in the Secretary for Justice

May 1999

June 1999

Government proposes a reinterpretation of the *Basic Law* from the Standing Committee of the NPC

The Standing Committee of the Ninth National People's Congress interprets Articles 22(4) and 24(2)(3) of the *Basic Law* and rules that "the interpretation of the Court of Final Appeal is not consistent with the legislative intent"

Appendix 4

Crisis: Opening of Hong Kong International Airport

October 1989	Governor Wilson announces plans for a new international airport for Hong Kong
February 1990	Airport Development Steering Committee (ADSCOM) established
April 1990	Provisional Airport Authority (PAA) established
September 1991	The governments of Britain and China sign the "Memorandum of Understanding Concerning the Construction of the New Airport in Hong Kong and related Questions"
1991	New Airport Project Co-ordination Office (NAPCO) established
September 1993	Head of PAA warns that airport will not be ready on time if China and Britain do not agree on the financial arrangements for the project
November 1994	A Sino-British deal on financing for the new airport concluded
June 1995	The Airport Committee of the Sino-British Joint Liaison Group reaches the Financial Support Agreements for the airport
	Target date for opening of airport extended to April 1998

December 1995	*The Airport Authority Ordinance* (Cap. 483) enacted and the Provisional Airport Authority is reconstituted as the Airport Authority (AA)
June 1997	Chief of HACTL (Hong Kong Air Cargo Terminals Limited) calls for a delay in the opening of the new airport because of construction problems
July 1997	AA under pressure as huge financial losses are predicted for delay in opening the new airport
November 1997	AA reaffirms airport would be ready for opening in April 1998
January 1998	Organisation of AA Management restructured on the advice of its management consultants
	Government announces 6 July 1998 as the opening date for the new airport
	Financial Secretary claims airport "will be completed on time and within budget"
June 1998	AA Chairman expresses confidence 10 days before its opening that the airport would operate smoothly
	A trial opening of the airport reveals major problems in the form of malfunctioning flight information displays and departure gates, long queues, slow computers, lost baggage
2 July 1998	President Jiang Zemin opens the new Hong Kong International Airport
	President Clinton flies into the new airport
5 July 1998	Airport at Kai Tak closes down and overnight convoy moves last pieces of equipment to the new Chek Lap Kok airportsite

6 July 1998	A number of problems leads to chaos soon after the opening of the new airport
7 July 1998	HACTL suspends air cargo imports and exports on passenger flights except for perishables, medical supplies and other vital goods and re-opens operations at Kai Tak Terminal 2.
8 July 1998	A computer failure allows a flight to Amsterdam to take off, carrying the bags of two passengers who had failed to board, contravening rules of the International Convention
	HACTL extends suspension of air cargo services at Chek Lap Kok for another 48 hours, costing about $3 billion for the 3-day ban.
9 July 1998	Legislators briefed about the airport crisis
10 July 98	An independent investigation into the airport announced
	Legislators propose to set up a Select Committee for its own investigation
11 July 1998	Airport Authority (AA) Chairman Wong Po-yan apologises on RTHK [a local radio station] for the chaos and accepts responsibility
	AA Deputy Chief Executive Billy Lam Chun-lung apologises on two radio phone-in programs
12 July 1998	A large number of sightseers flock to the airport to witness the chaos
13 July 1998	The Ombudsman announces the intention to conduct an investigation into the airport chaos
14 July 1998	ICAC arrests 12 people suspected of covering up substandard foundation work at the airport railway

15 July 1998	A Cathay Pacific jumbo jet collides with an airbridge, forcing the Airport to shut down its automatic guidance system for docking planes
16 July 1998	HACTL announces a four-phase recovery program
17 July 1998	Airport Consultative Committee (ACC) questions AA officials Henry Townsend and Clinton Leeks, and HACTL Managing Director Anthony Charter at a public meeting
19 July 1998	HACTL lifts ban on most imports and exports, but warns that operations would remain at 50% capacity
20 July 1998	Chief Executive makes his first visit to the airport after the chaos
21 July 1998	Justice Woo Kwok-hing and Dr. Edgar Cheng appointed by the government to conduct investigation into the opening of the airport
24 July 1998	Legislators visit the airport cargo area
29 July 1998	Legislative Council passes resolution to set up a Select Committee for conducting an inquiry into the circumstances leading to the problems surrounding the commencement of the operation of the new Hong Kong International Airport at Chek Lap Kok since 6th July 1998 and related issues
September 1998	A series of public hearings begins
	Chief of HACTL admits misjudging the scale of faults which affected air cargo operation at the new airport
October 1998	AA Chairman awarded the highest public honour for a Hong Kong resident - the Grand Bauhinia medal
November 1998	AA Chief Executive Townsend accused of misleading the government on the airport's readiness to open on 6th July

January 1999   Reports of the three investigations released

Select Bibliography

Apple Daily.

Arnold, H. J. and Feldman, D. C. (1986), *Organizational Behaviour*, McGraw Hill, Singapore.

Asian Wall Street Journal, The.

Asiaweek.

Baker, R.J.S. (1972), *Administrative Theory and Public Administration*, Hutchinson, London.

Berg, D. M. and Robb, S. (1992), 'Crisis Management and the "Paradigm Case', in E. L. Toth, R. L. Heath (eds), *Rhetorical and Critical Approaches to Public Relations*, Lawrence Erlbaum Associates, Hillsdale, New Jersey, pp. 93-109.

Bouckaert, G. (1993), 'Efficiency measurement from a management perspective: a case of the Civil Registry Office in Flanders', *International Review of Administrative Sciences*, vol. 59, pp. 11-27.

Burns, J.P. (1994), 'Administrative reform in a changing political environment: the case of Hong Kong', *Public Administration and Development*, vol. 14, pp. 241-42.

Businessweek.

Carino, L. V. (1992), *Bureaucracy for Democracy: The Dynamics of Executive-Bureaucracy Interaction During Governmental Transitions*, College of Public Administration, University of the Philippines, Philippines.

Carnall, C. A. (1995), *Managing Change in Organizations*, Second Edition, Prentice Hall, London.

Chan, J.M.M., Fu, H.L. and Ghai, Y. (eds) (2000), *Hong Kong's Constitutional Debate: Conflict Over Interpretation*, Hong Kong University Press, Hong Kong.

Charles, M.T. and Kim, J. C. K. (1988), *Crisis Management: A Casebook*, Charles C. Thomas, Springfield, Illinois.

Cheng, J. (ed) (1986), *Hong Kong in Transition*, Oxford University Press, Hong Kong.

Cheung, A.B.L. (1992), 'Public sector reform in Hong Kong: perspectives and problems', *Asian Journal of Public Administration*, vol. 14, pp. 115-48.

Chicago Tribune.

Commission of Inquiry (1999), *Report of the Commission of Inquiry on the New Airport*, Hong Kong.

Common, R., Flynn, N. and Mellon, E. (1992), *Managing Public Services, Competition and Decentralization*, Butterworth-Heinemann, Oxford.

Considine, M. and Painter, M. (1997), *Managerialism, The Great Debate*, Melbourne University Press, Melbourne.

Consultative Committee for the Basic Law of the Hong Kong Special Administrative Region of the People's Republic of China (1990), *Basic Law of the Hong Kong Special Administrative Region of the People's Republic of China.*

Daily Telegraph.

Denhardt, R. B. (1993), *The Pursuit of Significance: Strategies for Managerial Success in Public Organizations*, Wadsworth Publishing Company, Belmont, California.

Dimbleby, J. (1997), *The Last Governor: Chris Patten and the Handover of Hong Kong*, Little, Brown and Company, London.

Downs, A. (1967), *Inside Bureaucracy*, Little, Brown and Company, Boston.

Economist Intelligence Unit (1998), *Economist Intelligence Report.*

Efficiency Unit, Government of Hong Kong (1995), *Serving the Community*, Government Printer, Hong Kong.

Far Eastern Economic Review.

Fearn-Banks, K. (1996), *Crisis Communication: A Casebook Approach*, Lawrence Erlbaum Associates, Mahway, New Jersey.

Financial Times.

Fink, S. (1986), *Crisis Management, Planning for the Inevitable*, Amacom, New York.

Flynn, N. (1997), *Public Sector Management*, Third Edition, Prentice Hall-Harvester Wheatsheaf, London.

Government Information Services (1998), *Daily Information Bulletin*, various dates.

Gulick, L. and Urwick, L. (1937), *Papers on the Science of Administration*, Institute of Public Administration, New York.

Hargrove, E. C. and Glidewell, J. C. (eds) (1990), *Impossible Jobs in Public Management*, University Press of Kansas, Lawrence.

Harlan Cleveland (1992), 'The Twilight of Hierarchy: Speculations on the Global Information Society', in R. Denhardt and B. Hammond (eds), *Public Administration in Action: Readings, Profiles and Cases*, Brooks/Cole Publishing Company, Pacific Grove, California, pp. 366-71.

Henry, N. (1995), *Public Administration and Public Affairs*, Fifth Edition,

Prentice-Hall, Englewood Cliffs.

Henry, N. (1999), *Public Administration and Public Affairs*, Sixth Edition, Prentice-Hall, Englewood Cliffs.

Hong Kong Standard.

Hood, C.C. and Schupert, G.F. (1988), 'The Study of Para-Governmental Organizations', in C.C. Hood and G.F. Schupert (eds), *Delivering Public Services in Western Europe*, SAGE, London, pp. 1-26.

Huque, A. S. (1997), 'Public Administration and Infrastructure Development', *Hong Kong Public Administration*, vol. 6, pp. 1-9.

Huque, A.S. (1998), 'Disaster Management and the Inter-Organizational Imperative: The Hong Kong Disaster Plan', *Issues & Studies*, vol. 34, pp. 104-123.

Huque, A.S. (1999), 'Hong Kong's policy of positive of non-intervention: a critical appraisal of the 1998 stock market intervention', *Issues & Studies*, vol. 35, pp. 152-73.

Huque, A.S., Hayllar, M.R., Cheung, A.B.L., Flynn, N. and Wong, H.K. (1999), *Public Sector Reform in Hong Kong: The Performance of Trading Funds*, Occasional Paper No. 2, Department of Public and Social Administration, City University of Hong Kong, Hong Kong.

Huque, A.S. and Lee, G.O.M. (1996), 'Public service Training in a Changing Society: Challenge and Response in Hong Kong', *Teaching Public Administration*, vol. 16, pp. 1-16.

Huque, A.S., Lee, G.O.M., and Cheung, A.B.L. (1998), *The Civil Service in Hong Kong*, Hong Kong University Press, Hong Kong.

Huque, A.S., Tao L.P.W., and Wilding, P. (1997), 'Understanding Hong Kong', in P. Wilding, A.S. Huque, and L.P.W. Tao (eds), *Social Policy in Hong Kong*, Edward Elgar, Cheltenham.

Janis, I. L. (1989), *Crucial Decisions*, The Free Press, New York.

Kaufman, H. (1991), *Time, Chance, and Organization*, Second Edition, Chatham House, Chatham, New Jersey.

Kennedy School of Government (1998), *Coping with Crisis: Hong Kong Public Health Officials and the "Bird Flu"*, Case Program, C15-98-1430.0.

Kernaghan, K. and Langford, J. W. (1990), *The Responsible Public Servant*, The Institute for Research on Public Policy, Halifax, Nova Scotia.

Kiel, L. D. (1994). *Managing Chaos and Complexity in Government: A New Paradigm for Managing Change, Innovation and Organizational Renewal*, Josey-Bass Publishers, San Francisco.

Langford, J. W. (1987), *Fear and Ferment: Public Sector Management Today*, Institute of Public Administration of Canada and the Institute for Research on Public Policy, Canada.

Lee, G.O.M. and Huque, A.S. (1995), 'Transition and the localisation of the civil service in Hong Kong', *International Review of Administrative Sciences*, vol. 61, pp. 107-20.

Lee, G.O.M. and Huque, A.S. (1996), 'Hong Kong: Administrative reform and recent public sector changes – The institutionalisation of new values', *Australian Journal of Public Administration*, vol. 55, pp. 13-21.

Lee, E. W. Y. (2000), 'The new Hong Kong international airport fiasco: accountability failure and the limits of the new managerialism', *International Review of Administrative Sciences*, vol. 66, pp. 57-72.

Legislative Council (1997), *Report of the Select Committee to Inquire into the Circumstances Surrounding the Departure of Mr LEUNG Ming-yin from the Government and Related Issues*, Hong Kong.

Legislative Council (1999), *Minutes of Special Meeting of Panel on Administration of Justice and Legal Services*, Hong Kong, February.

Legislative Council Minutes.

Lerner, A. W. and Wanat, J. (1992), *Public Administration: A Realistic Reinterpretation of Contemporary Public Management*, Prentice Hall, Englewood Cliffs, New Jersey.

Lethbridge, D. (1978), *Hong Kong: Stability and Change*, Oxford University Press, Hong Kong.

Li, P.K. (ed) (1997), *Political Order and Power Transition in Hong Kong*, The Chinese University Press, Hong Kong.

Likierman, A. (1993), 'Performance Indicators: 20 Early Lessons from Managerial Use', *Public Money and Management*, vol. 13, pp. 15-22.

Liu, E., Lee, V., Wong, E. and Lee, J. (1998). *Matters Relating to the Opening of the New Airport at Chek Lap Kok*, Research and Library Services Division, Legislative Council Secretariat, Hong Kong.

Loh, C. (1999), 'Human Rights in the First Year—Genuine restraint or buying time?' in L. C. H. Cho and Y. K. Fan (eds), *The Other Hong Kong Report 1998*, Chinese University Press, Hong Kong, pp. 49-72.

Marini, F. E. (ed) (1971), *Toward a New Public Administration: The Minnowbrook Perspective*, Chandler, San Francisco.

McKevitt and Lawton, A. (eds) (1994), *Public Sector Management: Theory, Critique and Practice*, SAGE, London.

Metcalfe, L. and Richards, S. (1987), *Improving Public Management*, SAGE, London.

Miners, N. (1995), *The Government and Politics of Hong Kong*, Fifth Edition, Oxford University Press, Hong Kong.

Mitroff, I. and Pearson, C.M. (1993), *Crisis Management: A diagnostic guide for improving your organization's crisis-preparedness*, Jose-Bass Publishers, San Francisco.

Morris, J.(1997), *Hong Kong: Epilogue to an Empire*, Penguin Books, London.

Newsweek.

Office of the Ombudsman (1999), *Report of the Investigation into the commissioning and operation of the new airport at Chek Lap Kok.*

Patten, C. (1992), *Our Next Five Years: The Agenda for Hong Kong*, Government Printer, Hong Kong.

Peters, T.J. and Waterman, R.H. (1982), *In Search of Excellence: Lessons from America's Best-run Companies*, Harper & Row, New York.

Pinto, R. F. (1998), 'Innovations in the provision of public goods and services,' *Public Administration and Development*, vol. 18, pp. 387-97.

Pollitt, C., Birchall, J. and Putman, K. (1998), *Decentralising Public Service Management*, Macmillan, Houndmills, Basingstoke.

Provisional Legislative Council Secretariat (1998), *Minutes of Panel on Economic Services held on 9th March 1998*, Hong Kong.

Provisional Legislative Council (1998), Special Panel on Administration of Justice and Legal Services held 23rd March 1998, *PLC Paper No. CB(2)1492*, Ref: CB2/PL/AJLS, Provisional Legislative Council Secretariat, Hong Kong.

Rabushka, A. (1973), *The Changing Face of Hong Kong, New Departures in Public Policy*, A.E.I. Hoover Policy Studies, Washington, DC.

Reuters News Service.

Rosen, E. D. (1993), *Improving Public Sector Productivity: Concepts and Practice*, SAGE, Newbury Park, California.

Rosenbloom, D. (1989), *Public Administration: Understanding Management, Politics, and Law in the Public Sector*, Second Edition, McGraw-Hill, New York.

Rosenthal, U. and Kouzmin, A. (1997), 'Crisis and crisis management: Toward comprehensive decision making', *Journal of Public Administration Research and Theory*, vol. 7, pp. 277-304.

Rosenthal, U., Hart, P. and Kouzmin, A. (1991), 'Bureau-politics of crisis management', *Public Administration*, vol. 69, pp. 211-33.

Schneider, S.K. (1995), *Flirting with Disaster: Public Management in Crisis Situations*, M. E. Sharpe, Armonk, New York.

Select Committee (1999), *Report of the Legislative Council Select Committee to inquire into the circumstances leading to the problems surrounding the commencement of the operation of the new Hong Kong International Airport at Chek Lap Kok since 6th July 1998 and related issues*, Hong Kong.

Shapiro, I. (1994), "Introduction" in I. Shapiro, (ed), *The Rule of Law*, New York University Press, New York and London, pp. 1-10.

Shrader-Frechette, K.S. (1991), *Risk and Rationality: Philosophical Foundations for Populist Reforms*, University of California Press, Berkeley.

Simon, H. A. (1957), *Administrative Behavior, A Study of Decision-Making Processes in Administrative Organizations*, Second Edition, The Macmillan Company, New York.

Starling, G. (1993). *Managing the Public Sector*, Fourth Edition, Brooks/Cole, Pacific Grove, California.

Strait Times.

Terry, L.D. (1998). 'Administrative leadership, neo-managerialism, and the public management movement', *Public Administration Review*, vol. 58, pp. 194-200.

Tung, C. H. (1997), *Building Hong Kong for a New Era*, Address by the Chief Executive The Honourable Tung Chee Hwa at the Provisional Legislative Council meeting on 8 October 1997, Printing Department, Hong Kong Special Administrative Region Government, Hong Kong.

Tung, C. H. (1998), *From Adversity to Opportunity*, Address by the Chief Executive The Honourable Tung Chee Hwa at the Legislative Council meeting on 7 October 1998, Printing Department, Hong Kong Special Administrative Region Government, Hong Kong.

Vines, S. (1998), *Hong Kong, China's New Colony*, Aurum Press, London.

Wesley-Smith, P. and Chen, A. (1998), *The Basic Law and Hong Kong's Future*, Butterworths, Hong Kong.

Zinke, R.C. (1990), 'Administration: The Image of the Administrator as Information Processor', in H.D. Kass and B.L. Catron (eds), *Images and Identities in Public Administration*, SAGE, Newbury Park, California.

Index